The Song of Life

Lessons, Tips, and Insights for Healing You and Your Universe

George E. Samuels

iUniverse, Inc.
Bloomington

THE SONG OF LIFE
LESSONS, TIPS, AND INSIGHTS FOR HEALING YOU AND YOUR UNIVERSE

iUniverse books may be ordered through booksellers or by contacting:

iUniverse
1663 Liberty Drive
Bloomington, IN 47403
www.iuniverse.com
1-800-Authors (1-800-288-4677)

ISBN: 978-1-4759-7288-7 (sc)
ISBN: 978-1-4759-7290-0 (hc)
ISBN: 978-1-4759-7289-4 (e)

Printed in the United States of America

iUniverse rev. date: 2/15/2013

Table of Contents

Dedication

TO THE SUPREME MOST HIGH

AND LIFE IN THE UNIVERSE OF LIGHT

TO MY FAMILY WHEREEVER THEY ARE IN THE UNIVERSE

THEY ARE LIGHT

I AM!

Copyright laws apply

Introduction

The Meaning of Life?

The Song of Life is written to help those who need help or healing and have questions and seek uncomplicated clear answers. This is to help understand what else is there within their-own heart and minds. Others trying to understand their role in the world seek insight and information. Many people only see themselves and are not focusing on the universal, to explain un-answered queries they often ponder. When we move beyond our own mind and realize there is a universal mind you begin to see a world and a universe that you are part of, if not time to wake up. *The Song of Life* links the universe with you, and you with the universe, the universal consciousness within our own individual consciousness.

What does life mean to you? Is it you and no one else, is it you and the immediate family, is it your community, is it you and your state or country, is it you and all that exists on earth, is it all that exists in the universe? Are you ready to help all, recognize all or just you and a few friends? What does life mean to you? Is it breathing, eating, and providing shelter and clothes? Now that, you have done all that, what remains to be done, vacation, or a trip to Disney World? Do you now see beyond your needs, to include others? Do you consider what else there is in life that is seeking your attention? Is there something telling you there is more than we see or experience in our lives? Is there a chance there is more for you to do? Are you here for a special reason? Are you in touch with your heart? Does your heart reach out to others who need your help or advice or wisdom? Are you willing to explore the universal within? Can you see beyond the mirror?

In "*The Song of life*" you will find tips and insights to help you to gain valuable knowledge, techniques and support to propel you on to greater understanding of you and your universe. The lessons are making sure you can see your connection to more than what you currently see. Open and expand your vision to recognize the universe is more than a science project but an introduction to your universal partnership. Have you wanted to explore what is real, what is the truth, what is not, am I being told the truth or a lie and or do I want to know the truth. In this book, we explore the concept of truth versus lies, real versus unreal, visible versus invisible.

You are here now, are you healthy and happy? What does all this mean besides you surviving, each and every day? Are you being beckoned to realize that there is more for you to know and learn, and to gain that will lead you to a new higher level of understanding? Life means we are living, breathing and walking the earth at this time, and much is given and expected as we receive all we need and want while being called to understand more and go beyond the physical and material. There is a spiritual universal understanding we must understand and know about the universe and ourselves. This requires us to step out of our comfort materialistic zone. Look within and without to get a complete picture of whom we are. How do we see the universe as we explore all that is being revealed to us that exist in clear sight if we use our intuitive insight?

The Song of Life asks this question, are you healing or do you need to heal? We keep asking ourselves what does all this mean, and the answer is awaiting us if we only ask, seek and know, we will receive the answers we need. So what do we need to get started on the right path? The journey begins within as we take the first step. Of course, we must ask the first question, "who am I" then we are on our way. We will eventually reach the point when we will ask "why am I here" and reach the point of understanding that we are a part of the universe as our vision changes from me me me to us us us and we are the universe. *The Song of Life* takes us on a journey to the universe and the path is in front of us.

In *The Song of Life*, we begin to awaken a sense of the universal, the healing within you to let you know you are not done if you have not explored the universal and seen yourself, and as a part of the universe. Yes, you can heal you but stopping there you are not all done. I want to heal the universe, and we are a part of the universe, and we want the universe healed for all of us who realize we all are a part, realizing the Sun shines on us to awaken us to the light.

Life is a dichotomy of how do we handle the material and the spiritual. Some only focus on the material, others only focus on the spiritual, but all of us have to deal with both and balance how we live our spiritual lives in peace full of love and a need for nothing. The scales do not appear to be balanced, but it is our work to let go and understand the importance of this life of learning. We need to gain more of an understanding about ourselves, and the universe, where we live.

The Song of Life discusses many ideas, concepts and tools including meditation as a tool to assist us in our understanding of self, healing, the universe and all that is known and unknown. Meditation is utilized to turn our concentration from the outer world to the inner world within in order to contemplate how connected are we to the universal. Meditation is a technique by which we sit down, close our eyes allowing us to become quiet, relax, in order to create a level of concentration in order to receive esoteric information and insight. Later in the book we will discuss meditation further. At the same time, we will discuss energy and their importance within our inner universe. When discussing energy it is necessary to understand the chakras and their energetic system. In lesson twenty-two, understanding the chakras is vital in order to explain the life of a person's energy, how it is connected within and how that energy also is connected to the universe. Energy is everywhere, and we receive energy from the earth and the universe via the chakras. Understanding chakras are a book by itself, so I just give you an understanding of the chakras and further information can be researched at another time. Many do not know or realize that we are individuals who need to understand much more than we are given in the media or schools. We need to delve deeper to learn all that is available to us.

Many of us have come gifted, skilled and talented to survive and live exceedingly well, others have come challenged to rise above the mediocre and then some have come to help others to rise to the top. There are those who are here to insure you are walking in your truth and being you. At the same time, there are those here in service, healing all who are in need and want also to help heal the universe at the same time as they heal you. The universal is within us all, and we demonstrate this every day as a student of the universe or a teacher serving the universe in some way shape or form. We are here to make a better universe if we recognize whom we are.

The chapters in this book focus on how we interact on a daily basis, within our life, and the greater universal on some level. We hope these insights will help you to see you, in your place, in the spacious universe, and leads you to help others to as a part of the universal family.

We are being given many opportunities to see the universal in action through those things that go beyond our own experiences through wisdom and compassion. Realize our basic understanding is universal because we share the world together and basic things such as basic needs are universal. Many people sometimes forget and think they need everything to be about me and no one else, or I want it all. Yes, it is "survival of the fittest", but we need to remember it is about us all surviving and sharing the planet together. So universal thinking helps us to sort and inform us that we are universal and therefore, must not dis-include understanding the world as one of our ultimate goals in life.

The author George Samuels is an enlightened realized Spiritual

Master, Guide, Teacher, Healer, Spiritual Coach and Poet living in the San Diego area and is here to teach and help heal those who seek answers and to learn in order to help others. Master George has been providing Light, spiritual wisdom, healing, coaching and spiritual guidance for thousands of people throughout the USA and other countries for more than 30 years. He is continuing and is currently helping and healing all who contact him and are seeking Light on the Path. George has written several books of poetry such as *Audacity of Poetry, Healing in a Word, With Poetry in Mind, This is Our Word* and *There is Only Music Brother, Doors to Ancient Poetical Echoes* and *Lovers Should Never Quarrel.* His websites are www.spirituallifesource.com **and** www.gsamuelsbooksandart.com**.**

Our hope is that when you finish this book you will realize you can heal you and feel universal and embrace the fact that you understand, you are indeed a part of all this. Open your eyes to all who are a part of the same universe trying to co-create a better universe with you for all. We are all singing the same songs and listening to the universal rhythms. *OM! The Song of Life!*

Song of Life

Birds chirping
Water running
Bees humming
Mountains snowing
Life coming and going
Song of life singing a song
For who, all including those right or wrong
Thinking that there is, all there is
In their mind
Not thinking of mankind
We think we can find all we need to see
In the mirror, not you but only me
I look, I see
It is you or is it me?
I pass the blame
That all I see is the same
Flat is the world or is it just me
I can't look beyond to see
If I am part of the world to be
But I can hear the song they sing
Because the sound travels
Around the world like a circle in a ring
And life has a certain ring
I can hear the birds sing
The noise so loud
All is alive no doubt
The universe speaks to me
And whispers I am here, listen to me
For the world is round
And also in my heart, I have found
Because I care about all in my town
And I extend it beyond my breath
To reach out to us all, that I do care
About all of us, at home or wherever we are
For this world and universe we do share
And the plenty, for all of us, we hold so dear
So think life is a song
And we need all of us to take care
Of our family, community
And no one has immunity
For all is a part of this world
And the universe includes us all
To come and go, share and care
And help each other if we dare
To sing to each other
Helping each other through any strife
To celebrate, the song of life!

Lesson One:
You and Your Physical Universe

At a convention, I met Joe who came from a small town in middle USA. He looked lost since this was his first time in Los Angeles. It was the first time he had attended a New Age Spiritual Fair. He had an urging to attend and see why he felt the need to check it out. As he approached my booth, I saw he was nervous with a worried look on his face. I asked him why he was at the Fair. He nervously said, "oh just exploring". Then I asked him "who was he"? He states that his name is Joe. Again I asked him; "who was he? He bewildered said "I do not know". I asked him a second question; "why are you here and on Earth at this time"? Puzzled, he looked at me and said, "I am seeking to know that answer myself". I then stated that I was a spiritual advisor and could help him to find the information he was seeking. So we sat down, and I shared some information with him and also explained to him to meditate on the information he just received. Thanking me, he left to ponder the information he had received.

Why are you here?

Have you ever asked yourself this question? Has anyone asked you this question? Have you answered this question? Do you know why you are here? This question has been asked by thousands of seekers on the path to understand why they were born and what are they bringing to the world or what are they to experience, learn, and know in this lifetime. This is for the many people who have come to share their unique gifts with us, and the world. We benefit from these gifted people being here walking amongst us. We say everyone is unique, but it requires us to delve deeper to find out how special because many times it is not that apparent.

How did you arrive?

Yes, we all know you were born, and now you are growing or all grown up. So why are you here? What are you doing here at this time, this lifetime or incarnation? The answer lies within you, and you need to know the answer. One of the lessons is to learn who you are and why you are here. Once you know this then you can understand why you were born this lifetime and will possibly understand your destiny.

Everyone has a birth name, and as a person grows up they try to figure out why they are here and what they are going to do with their lives. The problem lies in what is the truth and what goes beyond assumption. Are you here for one reason or are you here for more than the reason you think. We need to know why we are here to insure we are fulfilling what and why we were born at this time. We are to know what needs to be accomplished while we are here.

So where do we begin?

First let's understand where we are and what we need to begin to learn. We were born to learn lessons and experience life on the Earth plane and have grownup after being nurtured by our parents, extended family, friends, community and local environment. This has caused us to think we are who we are, and why we are here. This has helped stabilize our life so we could grow and prosper in this life. For some, this is quite grounding, and for others there is always a question in our minds as to "is this all there is" or "am I only what I appear to know or is there more I need to know" or "is there more that I need to learn and understand". In everything we do, we learn about ourselves.

For some of us, we are truly satisfied not knowing anymore, and for others we feel we need to learn and know much more which for some appears to be driven by some inner yearning for more information. For others, they are on a quest, to learn the real meaning of their life. For we then ask the question again, why are you here? If you truly want to know, the answer lies within you and you must begin the search within you for that is where the answer can be found.

How do we begin?

You have asked the question and now need to learn the answer. For each person, there is a different answer, but different circumstances will lead you to the same place to ask the question, and you want "your" answer that is for you only. For us to understand and learn this answer we must first understand a few things that we should cover.

See life

Life is everywhere and in everything we see. When you look at things you should see life, living pulsating, breathing, struggling to grow as it comes and goes. As we travel around the world, down to the valley, up to the mountaintop, across the plains, in the desert, across the vast waterways we see all that exists, and it is all-alive.

What do you see?

So what do you see, what can you see and what is it that you do not see? This is a huge statement that needs to be contemplated upon and then questioned, studied and understood, as we perceive the answers. Look real carefully, do you see life, energy, breath, plants breathing, insects running and jumping, animals doing their business, fish flying and things we catch out of the corner of our eyes. We have to look more carefully to see all that was there or here but did not see at first sight.

Physical

The physical appearance we can see is so easy that sometimes we take it for granted thinking, is this all there is and negate even what we see to the point that even the physical (what we see in front of our eyes) becomes invisible. It is so magnanimous that we think we cannot take it all in and that we only need to pay attention to that which interest us. Then forget the rest, waiting for the immediate moment we need to see it.

Is that all there is? Do we negate the obvious and the obscure? Do we pay close attention to the obvious and closer attention to the obscure questioning why there is obscurity since some of us have expanded vision, to see much more if not all there is to see? Why do we only see a small portion of what there is to preview? Is this by design or the tunnel of our vision? Is it only what we can handle at this time until we are able to grow and evolve our eyesight to see more?

Some say we see what we want to see and no more. Is this the beginning of our ignoring what is in front of us or besides us or are we only previewing what we can comprehend at the time? Physically we can see as much as our mind and heart allows us to see. This assumes we are looking and wanting to know as opposed to, "I do not care to see anymore". So do we limit our own vision and relegate it to what physically we can see in front of our face?

Materialism

The physical universe created material, and we can see, feel, touch and sense it extremely easily. Most will say that it is all there is. Some call it the scientific approach and conclude that is all there is. Europeans thought the Earth was flat but that is because that was all they could see. When they decided to go beyond their limited vision, they found out there was much more and it also revealed that there is a multitude of things that are there, that heretofore they could not visualize. Many people say focus on the materials in front of your eyes and they then become attached to what they see as the material universe. They do not care or concern themselves with anything else. They can care less how we got the material, only that it is there and they can see, feel, touch, sense it and they can possess it for themselves as they begin to hoard all the materials they can find.

The belief that material only exist for them, and that they can possess it by any means necessary precludes the facts. In their brains, it only belongs to them under some unwritten rule. Grab all you can because all this material is ours and belongs to us, by any means necessary, some would say. But what is all this material, and who has made it, where did it come from, why is it here? There are those who will say, this is too many questions and state it just belongs to us, and we can have it, so what is missing? Who is all this material for? We know it is for us to live and use and enjoy in our daily lives, and we possess it just for that, and many do not care to know anything else. So what do you think about all of this, as we create more materials, more stuff and more toys?

Mind

When we say what do you think, we begin to go to a place outside of the material and beyond the physical barriers and delve into an area that is not by touch, feel, and the visual realm. This place is the mind and we are able to use this tool we associate with as the brain. We have figured how to use this ability called mind and continue to use it. Many connect the mind to the brain, but there are no visible connections we can point out. It is our first real hints that there is something beyond the physical that is invisible to the naked eye, and we have to use this tool to begin to understand what and who we are. Some find this difficult just as some find this easy, but most of us learn to use this invisible tool to begin to understand their physical world around them. I ask the question, can you touch the outer edge of your mind, can you see the mind, do you know where it begins and ends? Many people will ponder that question and reply with no answer. They only just think about it. The brain being a physical device has a multitude of functions. They are vital to life when we consider the nervous system and its functionality. The brain also does cognitive functions that reach beyond the basic physical function and intercedes between the mental functions that permeate our being, functioning every day on the physical plane and invisible to the naked eye using thought processes that emanate in our lives each and every moment.

We know or assume the mind exists but cannot qualify or quantify it. We take it for granted that it is ours, and all of us have this quality to use as required. To some, they view it as a physical tool and material substance (brain) and leave it at that. Scientist try to perceive but are stumped because they focus on the material and physical parts, namely the brain and stop there hoping no one asks the deeper questions that would cause them to go beyond the paper and pencil. Many also know that there is much more than the simple answers but are not sure where to go for the true answer and just speculate with the speculators.

Meta-physical

There are those who have "gone beyond" the physical to speculate that there is indeed this connection between the mind and the physical and that the two are naming it the meta-physical. They also conclude the two work harmoniously together connecting, what you see to also what you do not see. To some this is a leap of faith. They know it is the right answer, but others do not care to know the details just that it works that way. We do not need written proof delegating it to the realm of "what is" or "what if " like the chicken and egg theory. While others ponder monkeys as the intelligent evolutionary beings. When you begin to make the connection that we are meta-physical beings, you then realize the earth is not flat but also there is a universe out there to perceive. This is before you realize there is also another universe within your own mind that needs to be perceived first. You can utilize this knowledge to begin to understand much more than what is known such as the heart-love connection.

For all, we know the mind is the universe or is larger than the universe. To know this, we must explore with an attitude, and openness that the earth is round and so is our thinking. There are those whose minds are flat, and it can be discerned in their behavior, how they live and communicate with themselves and each other. There are those who do not want to know anymore, and we must respect their wishes just as those who need or want to know should be able to explore, learn and know more.

When we begin this journey of exploration, it resembles the explorers leaving home to venture out and see what else is out there beyond our physical sight. We begin on a different but similar path, but can go far beyond, and begin to be open to receive and perceive what else there is, that we should see and know. This is an epic journey that begins to lead us to a place we know not, but is all too familiar for us not to know. Question is can we perceive it all and can we learn all we need to know. What is there waiting for us to see or ask. Another question is this our real journey to go beyond to learn our true being, our true meaning in order to answer the question, what else is there to know. Stepping out on faith or a deep yearning we must learn more about whom we are and what is there for us to know.

Tips, Techniques or Insights

Explore your physical universe and begin with you. Look at whom you are, what, why and how you got to this place in time. Look at what you presently see and what you do not. Look at your life and jot down what comes to mind. Reflect on your local environment, where you are currently living. Reflect on what you think about your "present, living conditions, and how you feel about it. What keeps coming to you that you should pay close attention? Ask yourself this question, "is this all there is"? Is there more for me to learn and know? List the things you want to know or learn now.

Muladhara First Chakra Root Chakra

The root chakra is the grounding force that allows us to connect to the earth energies and empower us.

Lesson Two:
Family and You

The essence of humanity comes from the first man and woman that have bought us to this place via evolution in time. There are now billions of people who live and cover the Earth at this time. Are we whom we say we are or are we something greater? Does the sum of the parts equal to the whole?

Who Am I

Who are you? Can you answer this question? Yes, you can tell me your name without any hesitation and for most this appears to be sufficient. Again, who are you I continue to ask? What is the correct answer?

On the temple door it is written, "who am I"?

What does it mean and why do I ask? What is hidden, what is revealed? It is part of knowing who you truly are, and why are you here. Many people are being born at this time. They must learn to understand more about whom they are along with additional information, as to why they were born at this time. There are those who have tried to learn about themselves beyond what they can see in the mirror physically. They are gaining insight into information that will help them eventually. Am I the ego, or not the ego, namely who do I think I am. Am I some fancy title someone gave or told to me? Am I just this body or this mind? This is an essential step to learning or perceiving who you truly are.

So who are you, I ask again.

The answer is within, and when you ask the question you begin to look beyond the obvious, to understand more that is revealed when you begin to meditate on this very question. Seeking the answer will begin to open your mind to the possibly that there is more to learn about your life. For some, the answer will come easily, for some they will have to keep asking until they receive the answer and for others they will need some assistance to be able to get the correct answer. For most, this is about remembering!

Being You

In order to be you, you are requested to learn more about you. First you know the name that your parents gave you, and then as you begin to learn more and search for more information you are required to learn whom you are. Once that is completed you will begin to understand more, and you can begin to remember more that will help you to being and becoming you. Being you, will be one of the lessons learned that will provide an insight, and begin to assist you in explaining why you are here walking the Earth at this time. Many people wonder and question their existence because they think or sense there is more to know and remember.

You ask the question, how does knowing whom I am, will help me? Knowing who you are will provide information that will give you the ability to see and know more than you normally may have not realized, about yourself. This can make the difference between answering questions you had as a child or inner questions you may have that until now has not been answered. When many people receive answers, it helps complete those unanswered questions we seek. This can have a dramatically positive effect or affirmative agreement that they needed confirming. Have you felt like there was more in your life you needed to know and/or understand? The answers could provide a sense of satisfaction, completing an essential task that has finally been accomplished.

Ancestors and family

Who are you?

If you understand this question then you are on the way, but you must also understand more by understanding your family. Did you come here by yourself or is it the "immaculate conception"? The reason you are here has to do with family because everyone comes through a particular family. All who arrive have a family and that family in most cases can give you clues to who you are or who you have become. Why are you here at this time and what lessons do you have to learn. Families prepare you for what you need to learn or experience whether it is a positive or negative or neutral experience. The family you chose is ideally positioned to insure you learn or experience those events, or environmental factors that will provide you with the necessary foundation you will need as you learn and grow, and move toward your destiny. Many times we do not study our family to garner clues to whom we are or whom we are to be. We just take them as a given and determine if it is a great, good or bad experience.

Is That Our Family

Sometimes we feel as a part of the integral member of the family and other times we do not feel a part of the family. More important, we should discern what made us choose this particular family. This is better than blaming our family for whatever we feel is lacking or not compatible. Maybe the family needs you, or you need them. Yes, you chose that family and know this is a clue to learning more about you and what you are learning or why you are here or why your family needs you too.

Ancestors

Ancestors are the family that came before you and is your immediate family. This is if you have the honor of knowing your family. Ancestors were here before you and paved the way for you to be here so you should give thanks to the ancestors that you had the ability to come at this time. All have ancestors, contrary to what others may think there are no monkeys walking out of the jungle.

Relationships

Family also provides a clue into relationships because family is a relationship. Relationships are noteworthy because there are many types, such as friends, acquaintances, lovers, children, extended family, co-workers, colleagues and "strangers", but the first relationships created are family. All of these relationships are minor or significant influences in our life and help to shape how we handle our walk or journey through this life.

They say no man is an island because we are connected to family, friends, and others that help us through this life journey. Life is a journey, and we touch many people in our lives including family, friends and others whom we deem as strangers. Sometimes those strangers that have come and gone, we met or did not meet may play a part of our life journey. Because we may or may not know who is the friend or the stranger in our life, we need to learn to discern, who is who! Our family sometimes is small or as extensive as we know consciously or not.

Do you recognize who is who?

Have you ever met someone and said, "I know him or her", even though you have not met him or her before? This is because you know some people, even if you do not recognize them; you have met them on other life journeys in the past. There is much more to explore such as, have you met someone and felt you two have known each other, besides this chance meeting. That may be exactly so. For some, they question that while others believe in reincarnation or ask have we met in dreams. All of these are possibilities, but it does not matter your belief system. It just suffices to know it leave us with questions that need answers and further research. Its necessary to understand the connection between people you know and people you supposedly do not know.

Many people are connected together, and relationships will bring people together for a variety of reasons, but some of those meetings will bring you together with family and friends whether you know them or not. This does not mean every person is a family member or a friend, (smile). So discerning who is who is important because some people come bearing gifts? Some others come with masks on and you cannot easily see whom they are unless you look and listen closely!

Extended Family

We are born into a family, and that is where we begin. That family is our beginning, and it represents the microcosm of the universal family. We also in many cases have an extended family and some people have knowledge of this extended family and some do not. I always consider my extended family to extend around the globe. Many people though spiritual do not grasp this view of the world as their family, so they feel quite comfortable to separate themselves from those who are not directly connected to their local family. This is due to a lack of knowledge of the evolution of man and the entire family structure. Also, some people live with their extended families close or in the same house. In some houses, there reside three to four generations. Most people do not understand, but it is beneficial to understand the family of trees.

A single tree starts, and soon there are many trees and those trees transcend their local landscape, and when you see a forest, most of those trees were created and stem from that one tree. Then the rooting system connects and grows many more trees until you have a forest that expands beyond the local landscape and extends past the local state or country. If you do not believe go to the store and buy a bamboo tree, plant it and watch what happens in a short period to your backyard. Trees are not connected by a forest of trees, separate, and apart from each other. The trees understand clearly that its roots, and the rooting system connect the forest. The trees represent a branch and the branches of the tree represent the family of that tree. This should sound familiar as a man and woman have an off spring that creates a family. Then that man and woman also become connected to their families (in-laws) and so on, which can extend globally.

What does all of this mean? It means that we can have an extended family over generations that extend beyond our local family. Understanding this we should see other people in some cases as extended family members, to understand how we can connect to them even if we have not met them formally. This then will help us extend our hearts and vision to be able to see beyond our local sphere of influence until we reach the universe. This helps us to begin to ask again who am I and how do I relate to the universe. On the temple doors, it is written "man know thy self". It is crucial to know ourselves and then it does not stop there until we know how are we connected to others in the universe.

Tips, Techniques or Insights

Who am I? Am I me, the ego, the body, the mind or I am more than that? The ego may make you think you are many things, but you should understand whom you are. Meditate on this. Secondly reflect on your family. Begin with the ancestors; give thanks to the ancestors for all they have done to get you to this current place and point in time. Survey people around you, loved ones, relationships, friends, see if they have gained things from you. See what you have learned or gained from them. Ask yourself, are the people around you positive relationships or not. Ask yourself what are you learning from them.

Reflect how you have been helped to see how we fit into the world, and universal family. Also, how they have helped you understand your connection to the universal family. Ask who and why some of the people around you have come into your life. Are the people around you friends or not. If you feel anyone is not a friend figure out what you are learning from them or not. Then ask why have they come into my life. Second learn about you from history, meditate, ask those who are here to guide you to understand more about you.

Lesson Three:
Sensing (perception) Your Universe

When a tree falls in the forest does it makes a noise? I state this differently if a tree falls in the forest on your foot do you make a noise, and my answer is, you have to be there to know, but I'm listening. We listen to the noise but do not always listen to the quiet, small voice within us trying to advise us. If a person whispers the profound truth do we care to listen (in the forest) or to the falling tree?

Listening and Hearing

Are You Listening and Hearing?

Are they the same or is there a difference or is these semantics? Now hearing is of course associated with the ears as everyone knows and has experienced. This is step one, which, we call using the five senses. One sense is "hearing", and the other four senses are crucial. The other senses are feeling, seeing, smell and talking. These senses are vital within our everyday lives. These senses are indispensable when you begin to ascertain your ability to understand and experience higher spiritual gifts. Firstly we must sense the most basic of sensations.

Sensing our living environments and all who we interact with is step one but it is not all there is. Many say all is in black and white. Many scientists do not believe it if they cannot explain it via black and white, but there is so much they cannot explain so the scientist in many cases just discount certain phenomena knowing there is more than what meets the eye. The question is had we seen and heard it all, is that all there is? As we begin to understand there is more to learn, so we begin to explore senses that take us beyond the basic five senses. Some of us have been born with unique gifts in order to understand that which goes beyond the basic five senses. These extraordinary senses help us to see and explore what else there is.

We travel around the world, to learn that there is more than we have realized. As we learn more about the world our senses are heighten, we then have the ability to sense the world beyond and eventually the universe. These heighten senses can go beyond just seeing, feeling, and hearing. Our universe then ordered in our own minds now changes and expands and as we expand to take in more. We keep expanding until we realize we are a part of the universal, and it includes not only us but also everybody else at the same time. We start to sense or intuit that we are being exposed or led to seek more beyond our basic senses, and we want to know more. So we begin to research what if, and where is the knowledge we seek as we seek to know more. We search our skillset to see if we can figure all of this out. An inner urging taunts our curiosity and our intuition inspires us to help us learn more.

Intuition

Intuition is another skill or gift that most people experience, or sense or feel as a sense of knowing. This skill or gift can be a subtle feeling or, an extraordinarily heighten skill that provides the person with the ability to use these skills to help oneself. You can also learn to help others and sense more as we begin to go beyond the basic five senses.

Additionally we utilize one of the most critical skills or gifts called listening. Many people listen to others but fail to listen to their own self or inner urgings, which is there to assist each of us. This skill can be highly evolved and developed and then it can be utilized to receive information and insight along with valuable advice. This is called listening to the still small voice. Listening is considered a higher skill as compared to hearing. It is not that they are entwined both are equally indispensable. It is like the chicken and the egg, which came first. I'm sure there is a simple answer for that paradox, but most people are either not hearing or listening compared to those who do not know the answer. You have heard the statement "are you hearing?" or "are you listening?" We laugh and say, "I heard you". There are many who have demonstrated that they have higher hearing skills and gifts and can develop these gifts to help themselves and others.

Sensing the Universal

Hearing a voice, quiet, still voice, whispering to me, I wonder why? I look around, seeing no one I listen and look more carefully I hear the sound, the music, a tone, a bell, and a drum. I feel something, what did I just see, is it there, is it gone, did it appear? Some have heard of the faculty called the sixth sense that some people possess. This is not a mistake you are awakening to the fact that you have a gift, a skill that can assist you and others, and it is beckoning you to become aware.

Many people receive information with these gifts, and they can be developed to an extraordinarily high level called clairaudience. This gift called inner hearing is given to certain people to be able to discern higher inner knowledge and guidance. Listening implies that those who have this skill or gift are using it or paying attention to what information or insight they are receiving. Some people claim they can barely hear this inner voice, but this gift can be honed in order to improve there listening ability. Others cannot only hear but also can see or thereby see those things others cannot.

Seeing

Some people wear glasses and see well with them. Other people do not need glasses and can see just, as well. Also, some visually challenged people can see via visions. Then there are those who can see what others cannot see with their basic two eyes. This ability we called clairvoyance. The gift of vision is given to us to be able to see and is one of the five basic senses. The higher gift of seeing called clairvoyance is a higher ability, which we call a gift. This gift or skill is helping us to awaken to what is around us that others cannot see but is still there. This gift opens and expands our awareness. The universe is before our eyes if we look and some gifted people can see or sense that which appears to be invisible to others. Some thought the world was flat, now they know it is round. Some thought it was just our planet, now they know it is a solar system out there and every time we look we see more and more, and now see there are additional galaxies amongst the growing number of planets and stars. We can see ourselves in the mirror within if we look, or we can help others to see themselves with our gifts to help them understand what there is for them to see.

These gifts are utilized to see and discern what cannot be easily seen or discerned by the ordinary eye. These gifts are given to those who can utilize it to help themselves and others who need assistance in learning and gaining valuable insight. These gifts you are given are like other gifts used to assist you and others in seeking what cannot be ascertained by the basic five senses. These gifts amongst many other unique gifts provide a person extra senses that others do not have the ability to use. Special gifts are discussed in the future chapters as we begin to expand our senses and vision.

Tips, Techniques or Insights

First using your five senses see and hear what you have gleaned from this world and all that is around you. Ask yourself what do you hear, see, feel and sense beyond the five senses. What do you perceive beyond the five senses? Ask yourself do you have any extra abilities that expand your five senses. Do you see, hear, and feel things or sensations that give you additional insights to things, events, or extra ordinary information? Does your intuition give you insight to help or assist you and others? Do you listen to your intuition? Does it give you important and correct information?

Second determine which tools you have, which tools are fully developed. Determine what else you need to do through meditation, prayer and seek the guidance of a teacher who helps those to develop their spiritual gifts and talents. Its time, open the door to the universe, and see how you are connected to the universe. Then determine what is your purpose here. Time to go beyond the physical and observe all there is to see, hear, feel and experience that will let us know that we are all special to each other.

Lesson Four:
Meditating and Contemplating the Universe

Where am I? Is this reality or an illusion? Am I asleep or awake? How do I learn and know more? I will sit and let the Light show me what I am to see. I will meditate on all of this. I will listen to the universal.

Meditation

How do I contemplate the universe? First I must understand the universe. There are two universes; one is the micro universe and the second is the macro universe. The spiritual universe represents us in our inner glory whereby we represent whom we are in essence and how, that not only provides our substance, but then connects us to a similar extended universe, outside of us that extends to the beyond. We think we know it all, and maybe we do but if we do then we should understand that we must examine within first before we venture to the greater outer in search of what appears to be at home. Within we connect to the earth and at the same time we connect to the upper heavens as we fill the middle, (example of trinity). This middle is in balance and inside of us. We have to maintain an inner balance to keep us connected to the universe at large of which includes our connection to the earth. Inside we have a window to gain an insight into whom we are and our own cosmology that comprises the inner universe. Our minds and spiritual self let us have a way to see that we are more than skin and bones and affirm the universal that we are a part of.

The theories we hear and study are just an inkling into the important understanding that we need to gain, as to why we are truly here. This includes how we represent the universal and our spiritual relationship to the greater universal. It is essential that we turn inside our attention as we begin to look inside to the light within to recognize whom we are. We learn as much as we can, understand ourselves, and the universal, and all that this means in explaining our own life. Also, find out how are we connected to the world community, and beyond to the universe.

So as, we begin to ask the questions we need answered we need to seek the answers within, and not outside to verify that we are certainly part of the universal. This requires us to use the tools that are available. The tools given to us help us gain insight and wake up the mind and spirit. This includes information and knowledge of who we are and why we have come. One method is to use meditation which is a tool available to all to teach us to turn within and listen, look and feel that we are spiritual, light, love and universal. Meditation is a tool that can be utilized to provide inner access to the universal knowledge. Meditation for most is an essential requirement and needs to be done to help us when we need that key insight and verification. It is not the only tool but it is a simple tool that all can use. All have access to this tool and should apply it as much as they can or as needed to help us understand more about ourselves. This is one of the ways to fulfill the precept "man know thy self" written on the temple walls. Turning in helps us to focus away from the noise outside in our busy lives.

This sounds simple, but for some, they find it difficult to relax, but if this process is done every day the cumulative effect will be the ability to become quiet and begin the meditation process. It is also good to realize that it will take perseverance to accomplish this ability, but it will help you innumerable ways if you stick with it and continue the practice of meditation. This again is the beginning stage there is more to achieve, as we become more experienced at using meditation. There is much more to say, but it is essential that you must do your own work and gain insights and knowledge you need, so the experience is a personal one. Once you move beyond the basics, and begin to understand your inner universe, you learn how you are now connected to the greater universal. Then you will be available to assist others. Including contemplating that greater universal and what it brings to expand your knowledge of you and your connection to the universe of which we are all a part.

Tips, Techniques or Insights

So what can we achieve through meditation and contemplation? We can gain total awareness to the universal and begin to separate our understanding of the material and the spiritual, then how it comes together and at the same time see ourselves, as an individual and then through the duality of whom we are. Then, ascertain why we are whom we truly are as we begin to see that the inner universe as a part of that universal community that serves us all. This will shape our thinking to change from it is all about me to it is all about us!

You do not have to do anything unusual in order to meditate but sit down close one's eyes and relax. Begin to look within and listen to what comes up or happens, practice for 10 to 15 minutes per day to start. As we sit down, become quiet, relax and just calmly breathe we will begin the process of turning inside to begin to see within our inner universe. If you have problems becoming quiet, then you can focus on your breath and relax. There are many ways and types of meditation but when starting out you first want to be able to relax and become quiet. Choose a place where you can be undisturbed during your meditation. In order to succeed at meditation, you must do it regularly. Do not assume that doing it once or twice and giving up will work. Meditation is a lifetime practice so start and make it a part of your regimen. Becoming quiet is the number one objective, looking in is the prime directive, listening is required and being aware of what you hear, sense, and see is all a part of the experience of meditation. Write down what comes, so later you can decipher it.

Lesson Five:
This is Your Universe so
Expand Your Vision

Is your life wrapped around your daily activities trying to provide the essentials of life? Is your life surrounded around only what you can see with your two eyes or are you focusing on what is beyond your two eyes? Focusing, these are two distinctly different questions that illustrate two distinct views of what we may see in our lives. I look to the world and the universe, and while I also have to focus on the essentials of life I try to go beyond the smaller picture to the bigger picture that encompasses the universal thought. It is time that we look beyond ones own two eyes to see what else there is, and realize what is around us, and see beyond the trees and the forest. How can you and I do that? We can focus our vision on all that is around us and feel what is available if we extend our vision and insight.

Expanded Vision

Perceive what is around us, hidden or in full view. If we look and open our extrasensory senses that have been given, it will take us from our own perception to discern the universal. The universe is calling if one will listen. It is like nature that only ask that we see and listen and perceive what is in front of us and learn more about what it tries to show and teach us such as preservation, protection, love, sharing to name a few. The universe also has many more things to show and teach us and wants us to learn and experience much more. One must open, and expand their vision. Meditate on the world, on the universe, on all that is for us to gain and have insight. Contemplate more than ones navel, contemplate the world and the universe and look to the light that is within and without.

Responsibility

It is your responsibility to be aware of the universe even as we are aware of what we can see clearly with our two eyes. Others may tell you what is going on and what is around you, but you can also look and discern what is if you will only look, seek, aspire to know and be open to the Light. Whose responsibility is it they say, about everything. They say mind your own business but whose universe is this. Does any government own it? They may lay claim to the moon, but the universe has no flag, no quick claim deed, and if we do not accept responsibility man will say and argue about fault and who to blame. We are all members of the universe, and the rain does not discriminate like the Sun it shines its light everywhere, so we all have to look up and realize ones own responsibility to each one of us and to all. Remember nature grows food it does not say who should eat or who cannot. Only man does that while children look for meals or sleep hungry wondering why.

Tips, Techniques or Insights

Meditate and know you are expanding your vision within and then without externally. The spiritual universe is within, and so you are a microcosm and the universe is the macrocosm. See beyond the obvious. See the positive and the obscure. See what the universe is trying to tell you.

Helping others through selfless service is another way to take responsibility including helping, healing and teaching others. It is our responsible way to help each other to share this universe. People are the children of the universe, and those who think they, "deserve it all and no one else deserve" any, but them, are just misled or do not understand. It is your responsibility to open your heart and mind. Take some responsibility and know the universe is ours to share and many need our support on some level. We first have to be open, not close ourselves off and expand our vision to learn more about how we can understand the universal.

Lesson Six:
Gifts of the Spirit

Once upon a time a boy was walking in the desert wandering with his blue book. It was an extremely sunny day, and he had no money, nothing to do, so he looked around at the rocks and dust and thought to himself how he was tired. Coming up on a sizeable rock he decided to sit and rest a while, he was thirsty, but since he has nothing to drink he decided to take a nap. Just as, he was going to drop off, he wished he was rich, and all of a sudden a mirage of a mountain appeared. On top of the mountain, a man with a long beard appeared and summoned the boy. The boy astonished, thought how am I going to get to the top of that mountain, it cannot be real. As he thought, he appeared on top of the mountain in front of the old man. The old man welcomed him and asked him if he wanted to be rich. The boy said yes, and the old man summoned him to come in and follow him to a huge room. When the boy went into the room, the room was filled with diamonds. The man explained to the boy to take all he wanted and that it was ok. The boy started stuffing his pockets with one hand holding his blue book with the other, shoving diamonds in his pocket. The old man then summoned the boy to the next room asking him did he want gold and to take as much as he wanted. The boy was shocked and happily started shoving gold into his other pocket as the old man summoned him to the next room, asking the boy would he like precious jewels. The boy said yes, but he had a problem shoving all riches into his pockets and shirt especially since, he had his blue book in his other hand. The old man said to the boy to take all he wanted so finally the boy made a giant pile but could not carry it all so he put down his blue book and picked up all of the riches and then said to himself, "how am I going to get all of these riches down the mountain?" Suddenly he was back on the ground with a huge pile of his riches. The old man and the mountain disappeared, and the boy was now alone in the desert. Sitting on his rock with all these riches he was happy, but a little tired from carrying all the riches, so he decided to nap before he would try to carry the enormous heap of riches home. He took a nap, when he woke up he looked for his riches, but only saw a massive pile of sand in place of where his riches were. Shocked he became sad saying to himself, "someone stole my riches, or I took a nap and the old man took the riches back, I should not have taken a nap". He was now again broke in the desert and upset. He decided to go home, but he then looked for his blue book. It was nowhere to be found, and he realized he had lost his precious blue book. His blue book was filled with all his knowledge and wisdom, now he had nothing.

Using your tools to better Mankind

For those who have been given tools to help themselves and help others, it is a gift to show how the universal is helping all of us. The story above is a lesson to understand that even though people are getting all the riches, they should know riches come and go, but your knowledge, wisdom, and gifts, one should not lose for they are more precious. Material things will come and go, but your knowledge and wisdom will be forever, they are the true riches. They are universal and everlasting. Mankind should use its gifts and skills for the beneficial things and not only to spy and create conflicts or war.

Gifts and Skills

What is the difference between the two phrases? Gifts are bestowed by the Supreme (God Most High), and are given to an individual without having to give something in return. Gifts are also considered a natural endowment, a special ability, or capacity, or talent that a person possesses.

A skill is an ability coming from ones knowledge or learning or training or development. There are many people who have gifts and there are many people who have skills that they have learned or developed. Some have a combination of both which is when a person, for example, has what is called "raw talent" that is refined to a high level through professional training. The singing ability is such a gift because if that person did not have the raw talent they would not become a high-level talent or star. Another example, a carpenter can learn to become a master carpenter, but they may not become a master sculptor. A master sculptor can be born and sculpt with very little training and may never become a master carpenter. There are those who have the gift, the skill or have both, a sculptor and master carpenter as an example. A friend of mine is a sculptor and master carpenter.

Many people have gifts and skills, which are utilized to help others. Some have gifts but hide them thinking they have to keep it to themselves or use it for negative pursuits. Remember gifts bestowed upon you are for the positive use and growth of you and others you may help. Many of these gifts and skills or tools are universal in scope and are to help not only you but also others in the universe.

Gifts of the Divine

Gifts of the Divine are those bestowed upon particular people by the Supreme. We call these gifts spiritual skills that are to you by a Higher Power and you are taught how to use them. These skills are advanced abilities that some individuals have developed and can use them with little or no actual training hence why we call them gifts. There are approximately thirty-six (36) different gifts, but we will only briefly discuss a few listed below. For example, the following gifts or skills can assist one in the following:

Healing: the Supreme gives certain spiritual light workers the ability through whom God cures illness and restores health apart from the use of natural means.

Teaching: the Supreme gives specific spiritual master teachers the ability to communicate information relevant to the health and ministry of the Body and its members in such a way that others will learn."

Discernment: powerful ability given to many spiritual people to know with assurance, whether certain behavior purported to be of God is in reality divine, human, or not real or an illusion. With this gift one can recognize the true motives of people and also recognize when a person is distorting the truth or communicating error.

Service: an exceptional ability given to certain members as Light workers to perform numerous tasks related to God's work, and who make use of available resources and gifts to accomplish the desired results to help others.

Spiritual wisdom: spiritual teachers have been given the unique ability to know and give knowledge of Wisdom and Truth.

Miracles: this ability that is given to certain people that serve as human intermediaries through whom the Supreme performs powerful acts (miracles) that are (by witnesses) to have altered the ordinary course of nature.

Communications: an exceptional ability to communicate throughout the universe on every level passed to many spiritual masters

Prophecy: the unique ability Supreme gives to certain spiritual people to receive and communicate messages of God to His people to assist, warn, protect, heal and advise and etc.

Leadership: this ability gives spiritual masters the ability to lead and help the plans from the Supreme to set goals and the ability to work in such a way that they voluntarily and harmoniously accomplish the Supreme plans for his people.

Listening and hearing: this ability gives the spiritual person the opportunity to hear what other people cannot hear. It also gives individual people the ability to hear advice and guidance.

Transformation: a remarkable ability that gives spiritual masters the ability to transform energy and other forms in order to heal or create miracles.

Vision: this ability is unique, given by the Supreme and includes the ability to see what appears to be invisible to others and includes the ability to see through wall, dimensions

Compassion: this ability is to those who have the ability to give from their hearts selflessly and serve others by giving not only money but also service, help, assistance and in many other ways.

Manifestation: an ability to manifest spiritual needs given to help many people to obtain desired goals.

Transmutation: this remarkable ability gives specific spiritual masters the ability to transmute energy similar to the miracle to create gold from ordinary metal. This is also the gift of alchemy.

Universal knowledge: A remarkable ability that given certain spiritual people to discover, accumulate, analyze, and clarify information and ideas which are pertinent to the well-being of all."

Tongues: to speak to Supreme in a language that they have never learned and can receive and communicate a message of God to his people through a divinely anointed utterance in a language they never learned.

Interpretation: An exceptional ability that gives spiritual masters the ability for the Supreme to be known in the vernacular the message of one who speaks in tongues and can interpret tongues.

Tips, Techniques or Insights

Many gifts, skills, or tools are given to assist you in your development, and the ability to help and assist others. To determine what gifts, skills

or talents you have meditate on it and/or consult a spiritual teacher or advisor to confirm and assist you. If you have a guide consult your guide. Remember the story of the ten talents. If you have skills, gifts, and/or talents, use them to help yourself (in a positive way.) Learn how to use them to help others. We all are unique and have some gift, skill or talent to share with the world! In using these gifts, some training may be required, and remember practice makes perfect. Gifts bestowed upon spiritual people by the Supreme, are for the purpose (Divine Light) to help people and all mankind.

Lesson Seven: Discernment

Remember the story about the boy that cried wolf so many times that when a real wolf showed up no one believed him. They could not discern whether or not he was finally telling the truth. I remember a guy, my friends and I knew, who would tell so many lies that when he told us the truth, we never believed him. I met a lady that told so many lies, I asked her what happens if other people found out she lied and confronted her? She said, "she will just make up a new lie".

Lies versus Truth

What is a lie?

The definition of a lie is information or a story that is fabricated and not the absolute truth. Not many realize this. A lie is not the truth. A lie cannot become the truth. This is important because some in American philosophy think the idea that something can be true today but a lie tomorrow. Many so-called knowledgeable people state that they are telling the truth, but they are just fabricating so-called truths, which they know to be blatant lies, but think that since most people do not know they will accept a lie as the truth. This has caused substantial problems, wars, upheavals, distortions and genocide for many people throughout the world including events that are happening currently. Many lies are being told that are used to control people, deceive and distort many people's idea of the truth in order to subjugate them, rob them, take their homeland and control them through politics, and religion including those lies that support hate and bigotry.

This has caused above all mass confusion and continues to cause negative environments in every aspect of most people's lives because it is prevalent everywhere. Simple things like water, medicine, vitamins, processed foods: to race, religion, business, healthcare, insurance, unnecessary wars or the wanton stealing of peoples land and properties.

What for and why you may ask? Greed and control are the number one answer. Number two answer is ignorance and number three is foolishness. So many people have fell for a multitude of lies that were supposed to be the "truth" and believed these lies as the truth without questioning whether it was the truth or not. In some cases when they questioned the lies they were told (by so called leaders) they believed the lies even though they knew it was not the truth. There comes a time when you must stop following blindly, but question what is said to be the truth and not follow like sheep. The truth comes out in the end but even when some people find out the real truth they hang on to the lies they have been told because they have become the proverbial sheep, and only believe what they are told to believe. This sooner or later has to change when you are called to listen, not to the person lying to you but to your inner calling, which wants you to listen to a higher voice, a higher calling and to learn the truth about the lies you have been told so you can be aware of something called the truth. For example, the earth was never flat, robbing, looting, stealing and killing millions of people do not make you a savior or an explorer or i.e. seeking religious freedom, you are a criminal, murderer or warmonger.

Who lies?

Man lies to each other, and it is crucial to understand this when trusting men to tell you the truth. Why does man lie, there are innumerable reasons too many to address here, but there is no need, it is essential to understand this when sorting out or discerning the truth. So should you seek the truth, or just be satisfied with whatever lie everyone believes, and supporting because you do not want to stand up and be an individual. The real question is should you know the truth and if you knew the truth would you believe and change your perspective. So should you try to know the truth?

Truth

Is there such a concept as the truth? For some, they have not heard the truth, so they do not know how to answer this question, for others they have been lied to and do not believe anything, true or not. There are those who have knowledge of the truth but do not listen to it since they are accustomed to actively or passively supporting the lies that they know, or question as to whether it is a lie or the truth. Then there are those who seek the truth and listen. They also recognize the truth.

What is truth?

The definition of truth is the verified or indisputable fact, principle, reality or actual state or character of being true. We have all heard the statement "know the truth and the truth shall set you free". I say tell the truth, and you will be free. This means that there is such a thing or concept or statement as the truth, which will stand up over time and will be factual now and in the future.

Can you handle the truth?

Most people realize that the concept of truth is so powerful, so huge, so real that they sometimes feel it is too much for them to handle, and it is such an awe awakening they are overwhelmed, and it may or will change too much in their life. This will not change the concept of the truth, but there are those who upon hearing it run and hide hoping it will change and for some they are hoping that someone will (continue to) lie to them or hide the truth rather than face it.

So should you seek out the truth, yes? There is an ancient saying that states: "seek and you shall find", is also another statement: "know the truth and the truth shall set you free". I say the truth is only one story, lies a million stories, too many to remember. The truth is essential when you realize that there are truths to be sought, heard and learned. There are those who are called to hear the truth, seek the truth and to find out the truth. These seekers are important because they will not settle for just lies and they even when told lies want to search and discover the truth. This seeking whether it is an inner-urging or intellectual investigation is worthwhile and will help not only the seeker but also, others who are also searching for the truths about a variety of subjects. For some this is like searching for the forest through the trees and it is not as easy as it seems to appear. It does require seekers to search, research and try to clear away what is hidden or obscure to many but available.

There are obstacles that you have to overcome, some very minor, some major and most available for the true seeker. This will for some require you to clear away some lies, some illusions and begin to try and discern what is real, a fact, lies or truths. So what is stopping us from having readily available the truth about any subject we request or require? Well that is a book by itself, but most of the problems are about the truths we seek are either obscure or covered in lies and illusions, to keep you from knowing the truth for a variety of reasons, too many to list here. The truth lies within you, believe or not.

Illusions

The truth many times is covered with a veil of a multitude of illusions that have been created by a body of lies, told to cover up the real truth, so that an individual(s) can use these illusions to take advantage of an individual or groups of people. Over time, many lies have grown to the fact that it has created such an illusion (and the real truth hidden) that it is hard to find or clarify the truth because the people being lied to will not or refuse to believe you. Some do not care about the truth.

Some illusions are simple but profound, but can be easily dispelled by sincere seekers who are willing to search for the truth, and will not allow the illusion of lies stop them. Some illusions, no matter how great they appeared to be, were dispelled eventually because they were lies, and there was no facts supporting them. For example, "the earth is flat", "Iraq is going to attack the US and have weapons of mass destruction", "the picture they show of Jesus Christ is the real Jesus", and we know what the dinosaurs were doing during their age or people with larger size brains are smarter. There is much more, but the importance here is to explain to the real seekers of truth, to seek the truth. Start with one-self, and begin to learn all you can about your own truth. Begin to seek the truth about the countless lies, and illusions we deal with on a daily basis. Focus on you first than the rest of the world.

Seeking the truths we need to know to grow is more about the fact there are truths that we need to understand and know about ourselves the world and the universe. This is a positive approach to improving our self first then being able to help others and the world. Everything starts with you so knowing this we should start right where we are. That is the best place as we learn to discern what it is that we need to know and understand.

Such questions will come to your mind such as "who am I", "why am I here?" what is real, true and what do I need to know so I can grow, and be the best I can be!

This will begin to lead you on the way to learning more then that appears to be obscure. We need to understand and discern more about what is true and not true. It may help you climb through the veil of illusions that seem to be around you until you decide it is time to know more about what appears to be a lie, and what appears to be the truth.

IS anything true?

Of course, that is for you to find out, for you to learn and discern it but will require you to seek, ask questions, and you will eventually know! Some will say there is no truth, but that is what you need to seek, discern and confirm for yourself! Ask yourself, what do you believe to be true? What have you thought to be true that you found out later it was not the truth? What is it you thought was a lie but later found out it was the truth? These are the things that make us examine what is true or false, real or not real or surreal. What do you do if you want to find the truth? The truth is there for you to know, but it requires you to do the research, and then confirm that your research is valid and has revealed the truth to you.

How does one seek the truth?

This is done by utilizing tools; given to individuals, who are true seekers and are led or guided to look beyond the obvious and try and learn more. This begins with research, reading, listening, meditating, contemplation, and using many other gifts that are given to those who are given the gifts of discernment.

Seeking the truth is for some, a lifetime journey that assist you to find what you are seeking. For others, it will require sitting down and listening within when doing your meditation. For others, it will require seeking a Teacher who can give you valuable information or a guide. For many, it will require inner research to find out the truth. For others, it is considered an extraordinary journey when one is dedicated to going beyond the status quo to seek the truth. You can succeed in your search if you truly and sincerely seek what it is you are searching for, but you need to ask if you genuinely want to know! It will require you to clear away the gross lies and impediments that are in the way but there is light at the end of the tunnel. This will also require you to utilize advanced skills, gifts and research in order to discern the truth from those that masquerade lies considered truth but are not the truth. It is a worthwhile pursuit. It is nothing to fear, only to learn and understand. This all leads to the ability of discerning, that which, is vital but not so apparent to others.

Discernment

What does it mean to discern or discernment?

Can you see right from wrong, truth from a lie? Can you discern the reality from the illusion? Can you discern the truth? To discern, means to perceive by sight, or some other sense, or intellect, the ability to discriminate or distinguish the difference between right and wrong, true and false.

Discernment is an ability that is given as a gift to those seeking to go "beyond the obvious" to determine what is true or false or right or wrong. This is required because so much of the truth is hidden or disguised so that many people cannot readily find out the truth, without help. The reason is that man has created environments that sometimes mask what supports their own gains. These gains can be for ignorance, greed, power, control, and a host of other reasons that are again too numerous to explain but it is vital to understand so that you will realize the importance of your search or journey to seek the truth. The truth is available for all to seek and know.

Do you already have the tools to discern the truth?

Yes, you all have these tools but if you are not already using them, and they are dormant you need to activate them and begin to use them with or without the help of others. The real question is can you see right from wrong, truth from a lie, can you discern the reality from the illusion. There are many tools given to you to learn to discern the truth. The basic tools are called the five senses, above the five senses there are gifts and skills that give one extra-added perceptions that are called sixth and seven senses. One of these is the gift of intuition that assists us to know what is true and not true including what's right and wrong. This is partially what is considered to be gifts and skills that are from your higher self and the Divine or spiritual levels.

So how do these tools help you?

This is the fundamental requirement to be able to discern what others do not see, or hear, and feel with the ordinary senses, but requires those who seek higher information such as truth to go beyond the physical appearance. These advanced skills given as gifts assist the seeker to be able to accomplish their many tasks of discernment. Can you see the moon turn, can you hear the ocean move when it is still, and can you hear the tree in the forest when it falls? Can you tell the time without a watch, can you see the invisible, can you feel the breeze when the wind does not blow? Can you hear the chime when it is not ringing, can you hear the bell when it is not around, can you beat the drum when it has been moved to an unknown location? Can you feel the energy move?

These questions are just to make you think about the possible and the impossible. What is possible and what is impossible? Sometimes the lines are clear other times the lines are blurred. In order to see clearly, you need an extra ordinary skill that will assist you to begin to go beyond what appears to be impossible, and become possible. In order to discern the indiscernible to the naked eye you need special tools, skills or gifts. Then you will have the ability to discern and understand those things or concepts that appear to be hidden but available to the true seeker.

Tips, Techniques or Insights

Do you tell the truth all the time? Do you lie thinking it helps the other person, thinking they cannot handle the truth? Do you lie to yourself about the truth, or situations in your life, thinking it will make things easier to deal with? If so then you need to change. Start telling the truth. Lies do not make it easier; it only makes you a liar. If you want to walk the path of truth you need to tell the truth. Ask yourself are you living your truth if yes great if no then ask how to begin walking and talking and being the truth so you can see the truth in you, the world and the universe. This will help you to see the difference between the lies, the truth and illusions and what's real. We all have the ability.

Learn to discern the truth. Develop your power of discernment, do research, listen carefully, investigate, meditate, do not allow fear to keep you from seeing or hearing the truth. Do not fear the truth. Know your truth, decide what you know or do not know, research, determine what is the truth of reality versus illusion. The truth will free you from the illusion and help you to walk your path of truth.

Vishuddha Fifth Chakra Throat Chakra

The heart chakra is considered to be the love center

Lesson Eight:
Mental Universe

Many friends have told tell me that the worse case scenarios they imagined, actually happened, I wondered why this was? I told my friends that thinking the wrong thoughts, thinking of the worst, expecting the worst, expecting it, it could happen. The flipside is I have friends who have imagined the best and the best actually happened, and I wonder why this was? This confirmed to them that the best could happen. It is all in your thoughts. This helps us to understand the concept of "thoughts are things" and the importance of controlling our thoughts or what we are thinking.

Positive thinking

What are you thinking right now? What have you thought about in the past? Has it been more negative or more positive? Have you had negative and positive experiences? Sometimes we experience many things, or as some would call it trials and tribulations, we do not always understand the reasoning behind those events or how our mental inner and outer universe is involved. The mind supports and controls our mental thoughts. You may have heard that thoughts are things, but many people do not believe its true due to the intangibles of the mental, and the thinking faculty is not merely physical in nature. So it cannot be touched and felt or seen by the naked eye. The mental inner universe of our mind holds the framework of our thoughts which lets us ascertain our interaction with our three dimensional environment. People have total flexibility in their thoughts to think whatever they like whether it is negative or positive. We assume that when a person thinks proper thoughts they are thinking correctly and when a person thinks negative thoughts that they are not thinking correctly, but in our understanding of our inner universe we will not judge what is correct or incorrect in a persons mind. We will discuss how thoughts affect us within our own inner universe and how it affects us in the extended outer universe.

Positive thinking refers to our mind thinking thoughts that will assist us in our ability to do things beneficial to our own wellbeing. When it comes to health, we should be thinking what makes and keeps us healthy and in balance. For example, I think that I am healthy and that my health is improving every day. It will create a positive effect within my own mind. This can be translated into my not causing undo stress or worry about my health. If I think that people are following me even though I do not see anyone, but it is in my own mind, I will most likely react to this thought and act out in a paranoid manner. What mental processes are connected to my inner and outer universe such as listed below?

* my thoughts
* my health
* my life
* my family
* my work
* my relationships
* my activities

What positive mental processes or thoughts cause these outcomes:

* Happiness
* Love

* Peace

* Tranquility

* Sense of safeness

* Freedom

* Wellness

What negative mental processes or thoughts cause these things listed below:

* Stress

* Tension

* Paranoid

* Over-excitation of my energy

* Loss of energy

* Stress on health and the body system namely organs

* Secretion of excess hormones

* Reaction to external events involving others in my local environment

* Stress on personal relationships

* Mental fatigue

* Judgments

* Worry

These are only a few examples that will lead to the cause or solution of problems and challenges in our mental universe. You have heard others discussing the mentality of looking at a half glass of water and whether a person is optimistic or pessimistic (thinking positive or negative). This analogy is better utilized to understand how we think in a certain way. This also shows how our thinking has an impact on our psyche, our consciousness and how it translates to our mental reality. Ask yourself do you always think the worse? Do you think the best? Has your thinking been shaped by others to being neutral or negative or positive? Do you analyze your own thoughts? Do you ask yourself questions as to why you think a certain way on a certain subject no matter what it pertains to? Have you asked yourself, just what am I thinking, on any particular subject, whether positive or negative? The reasoning behind the self- discovery when asking and answering these questions is only for your insight and to assist others in determining their thinking and their thought process. This is not a discourse in blame but a way to utilize investigational type questions to provide an insight and understand their effects on us, and how it affects others.

For example, many people think that if they worry all the time it will help a given situation. In actuality, it causes us to lose energy and overtime affects our internal organs. How does this happen? Understand where our thoughts and mind go so does our energy. This will eventually keep us in balance or throw us out of balance. At the same time if we realize this we can change our thoughts, and it will help us not to dissipate our energy worrying. It will help us to stay in balance thereby releasing any tension in our mind, internal organ and body system.

Negative thinking

In every situation, there is a negative, neutral, or positive thought, which surrounds that event or circumstance. If we think or determine that our thinking is considered negative, we have the mental capacity and ability to examine our own thoughts, to determine if we are thinking correctly on that particular situation. Then you can either be satisfied with your thoughts or change your thoughts around that given situation. It is important to know we can think and control our thoughts at the same time as we can control the steering wheel of the car as we drive down the road, or steer our bicycle as we navigate through the streets. Understanding our thoughts helps us to understand ourselves on many different levels and in many different environments, and situations affecting our individual selves, and within our interaction with others. If we are thinking private thoughts that affect others in our inner mental universe it will eventually affect others in our external universe so we should be cautious on how we use our thoughts especially when it pertains to others.

Thinking negative thoughts may sway our actions in a negative way when we plan to express ourselves in a positive or different manner. The thinking of negative thoughts may also cause a negative not so desirable impression on our mentality that eventually manifests itself and then we will wonder how we got to that point, not fully understanding it was our thinking that ultimately created this unlikely situation.

The good news is that we all can change our thinking.

As a man or woman thinks

Men and women have the same talent in their mental universe within so we can use our minds to think the thoughts we prefer that make us feel comfortable. Our relationships depend on this, and we should know our thinking does affect our relationships. For example, it is known that the mind affects the blood pressure of a person, but it also affects their relationships with other loved ones close to us. So we have to be the controller of our own thoughts.

The mind as the controller

When we hear the words relax, or calm down, whom are we talking to? We are talking to the mind of the person and that person will direct his mind to think calm or relax so that the energy and body will follow suit. The mind will think of a thought and the body will react accordingly to the instructions it has been given. The instructions come first through the mind then to the brain to perform any specific instruction or activity. So remember you control your thoughts and your mind.

This will help us especially when dealing with ourselves as well as with others. If you do not want a certain thing to happen or a certain undesirable outcome then the first thing you must do is change your thinking to the outcome you want to happen. I have an old saying, "thinking it, it happened". Thinking the right thoughts will produce the right results most of the time.

The mental universal thought process

The thought process is a way of thinking that we can preview and/or view while it is happening. Many people should listen to the words that come out of their mouths as a way of understanding what you are saying. This will explain how thinking controls what we not only think but what is uttered from our mouths. This also tells us we can look at what we are thinking before we say anything. Our thoughts being private and invisible to others is available to us, and we can determine what it is that we are trying to convey, and articulate when we speak, and interact with others so that we are perfectly understood. This also gives us the opportunity to open our minds, and look at our thought processes, similar to the way an engineer or designer views and analyzes their thoughts before expressing them in their works. If we do not receive the desired outcomes or results then examine our thoughts.

The Artist within

The mind is a true artist because all the things that are being manifested are first formed in the mind then recreated in the universe, for us to view or experience. The painter does not first paint, he or she first imagines the very image in their mind, the carpenter first sees the chair in their mind and then fashions it from his mental picture or vision. Our imagination is in our mental universe and helps us to creatively utilize our minds to create wondrous things and innovations. From that mental process called imagination we can create many useful products, help others to accomplish their tasks and use our minds to influence the external universe in a positive way.

The positive mental process helps to transform our world and helps to keep us healthy, and through this we are able to help others. Not all the time are our thoughts positive, so with the same mental tools one can think thoughts that are not positive or advantageous. Recognizing this on their own or with the assistance of others we can recognize this kind of thinking, and develop change within us, thereby transforming our relationships and us.

Why should I think of the mental universe? It is a part of all of us, a persons' thinking, vis a vie thoughts that can affect not only our own self, but can affect how we express our individuality and community. We are all in the same universe so what we are thinking of doing can have a bearing or effect on all of us. When men and women think good thoughts, it is tantamount to creating good outcomes, good and healthy relationships and positive reactions to otherwise situations. This keeps us from blaming others, for our thoughts that appear to be destructive, and causes us to be suspicious of everyone including those with good intentions, only to realize at a later date, it was our own thinking that was wrong and needed to change to have a positive outcome.

Tips, Techniques or Insights

As healers or light workers remember to sit and think about what you think, are your thoughts positive or negative. Do you think you can or cannot? Do you visualize positive things, outcomes? Do you think about what you want to accomplish in your life and what you want to happen. Think of success, when thinking about goals. Visualize yourself succeeding at your tasks and goals. Think not, what you do not want to happen. It is said that it starts in the mind so remember this and think positive thoughts about everything including relationships and your work. Let go and dismiss any negative thoughts now. Think and affirm healing thoughts.

In the healing practice, it is imperative to ascertain what a person is thinking and what is happening in their mentality in order to assist them in their ability to be and remain in balance both mentally and physically. Many times our understanding of our self and/or a client can greatly improve their wellbeing. Destructive thoughts held in the mind for long periods of time can adversely affect one's health and wellbeing. This requires us to help our clients to release their thoughts or beliefs, determine whether right or wrong, change their minds and achieve equilibrium within their own mental universe. This can put the client and us at ease and be a catalyst for positive outcomes. Think and affirm healing and positive thoughts.

Mandala

Lesson Nine:
Affirming the Positive

Should I send negative things? Should I think negative thoughts? The answer is no for both questions. Remember as we discussed earlier, thoughts are things, and how you think is most important. Many people need a little help to change their thinking to be positive all the time. When we affirm the positive it puts us in the frame of mind that keeps us positive. Thinking the positive of what we want to happen can be done by thinking positive, in our prayer, and affirming it silently or verbally.

Affirmations

Affirmations give us the ability to affirm positive and divine statements that will help us in accomplishing positive tasks and achieve positive goals. Whether its things in our everyday lives or personal esoteric goals we want to accomplish. Affirmations can be created for nearly anything we want to focus on, model, create, remember, or change. Examples such as "be positive"," think good thoughts"," I am a winner", "I give and receive love" to name a few.

Create affirmations that will help you, place them on the mirror, on the fridge, in the car or anywhere to remind you of anything you want to remember. There are affirmations that are spiritual and assist us with our inner growth and helps to assist others with their own growth and understanding. You can recite affirmations repeatedly to remember them. These types of affirmations are called mantras.

Mantras

Mantras are sayings, invocations, spiritual words or sounds and vibrations that have been passed down by spiritual masters to assist people in their inner growth in order to accomplish their esoteric and exoteric goals. There are extensive mantras that are connected to every spiritual and religious dogma and some follow very spiritual traditions. Most mantras have esoteric meanings and one should know what they mean before reciting them, and also know why you are reciting that mantra. We only recite those that will help you or others, so it is good to know what we are reciting.

Many religions have a variety of mantras, but most are familiar with the Vedic and Buddhist traditions and represent spiritual sounds to help with inner growth and transformation that help seekers with their spiritual growth. We are familiar with "OM" pronounced AUM and many mantras are connected to vital sounds that are reverberated within the universal. Mantras are recited over and over so that the sound can reverberate throughout the universe. Some mantras are considered the sound of the universe such as the word "OM" pronounced "Aum".

Healing Sounds

Mantras also can be used to heal people due to certain sound vibrations, and can transform people by the practitioner reciting sounds or the healer utilizing certain sounds on the client that will effectively assist the person in their healing process. In Chinese medicine and Qigong healing sound vibration has been used with much success. Traditional sound therapy has been used from bells, singing bowls, and drums to music. When a healer recites healing sounds they will help to heal, but the client can also use the healing sounds to heal oneself. Qigong masters know how to use the healing sounds to heal by using certain sounds to heal specific dis-eases. These sounds are pronounced and repeated out loud by the practitioner or the person needing the healing.

Below is an example:

* 嘘 XU [pronounced like 'she,' with the lips rounded] - 'deep sigh' or 'hiss' - Level the Liver Qi

* 呵 HE [pronounced like 'huh'] - 'yawn' or 'laughing sound' - Supplement the Heart Qi

* 呼 HU [pronounced like 'who'] - 'to sigh,' 'to exhale,' or 'to call' - Cultivate [or Shore Up] the Spleen/Pancreas Qi

* 呬 SI [pronounced like 'sir'] - 'to rest' - Supplement the Lung Qi

* 吹 CHUI [pronounced 'chway' or 'chwee,' depending on locale] - 'to blow out,' 'to blast,' or 'to puff' - Supplement the Kidney Qi

* 嘻 XI [pronounced like 'she' with tongue high and well forward, in the mouth] - 'mirthful' - Regulate the Triple Burner Qi

All syllables are pronounced on a level tone - the so-called first tone (regardless of the dictionary pronunciation of each word); typically all but the fifth sound are sustained - the fifth sound may be sustained, or pronounced quickly and forcefully. (Wikipedia)

Mandalas

A mandala is a drawing that is considered to be a three dimensional composite diagram used as a meditational aid. Mandalas are being used also as a contemplative aid for meditating people to envision a three dimensional vivid image to lead them to enlightenment. There are many types of mandalas. As a meditative tool in Tibetan and Buddhist traditions Monks create "sand mandalas" to explain impermanence by sweeping away the "sand mandalas" once completed, then prayed upon and invoked with positive affirmations and finally swept into flowing water to be shared with all mankind and the universe.

Power of Prayer

Prayer is an invocation, affirmation, request for divine help, a rapport, requesting assistance, and a way of worshipping to a Higher Source or Divine Higher Power to hear your supplication and help or assist you with your needs. It is also used to give praise as a form of worship. The power of prayer is known and considered sacred and should not be overlooked or minimalized. It can be very powerful and can assist the one in achieving their needs and to help and assist others included in your prayer. It should be utilized for positive objectives and results. Also the power of prayer can be done by writing to the Supreme.

Tips, Techniques or Insights

"The mantra Om Mani Päme Hum is easy to say yet quite powerful because it contains the essence of the entire teaching. When you say the first syllable Om it is blessed to help you achieve perfection in the practice of generosity, Ma helps perfect the practice of pure ethics, and Ni helps achieve perfection in the practice of tolerance and patience. Pä, the fourth syllable helps to achieve perfection of perseverance, Me, helps achieve perfection in the practice of concentration, and the final sixth syllable Hum, helps achieve perfection in the practice of wisdom. "So in this way recitation of the mantra helps achieve perfection in the six practices from generosity to wisdom. The path of these six perfections is the path walked by all the Buddha's of the three times. What could then be more meaningful than to say the mantra and accomplish the six perfections?"

— *Dilgo Khyentse Rinpoche,*
Heart Treasure of the Enlightened Ones

The six perfections are as follows:

Generosity – giving in many ways from the heart

Ethics – how we treat each other, proper moral behavior and commit duties not harmful to others, not committing negative actions toward others

Patience – means the practice of patience, staying calm, showing compassion, slow to anger

Enthusiastic Perseverance – *performing virtuous actions, not giving upset at failure, if you fall down get back up*

Concentration – *meditation and ability to do one pointed concentration*

Wisdom – *transcendental wisdom, omniscience of the knowledge of every aspect of reality and knowing*

The essence of most mantras is to affirm positive ideals and clear away negativity. If you want to recite mantras you should listen to a Spiritual Master or Teacher to advise which one is best or you can utilize the ones that are given to you within your meditation or are guided to use. You can also learn more about healing sounds and how they are used to heal. Remember sounds create vibrations that can move energy, which helps to prevent and open blocks. Also do not forget to use the positive power of prayer. Strive to be perfect!

Mandalas are created by Monks and Healers as healing tools to help heal all in mankind and are extended, to the world and all who view the mandalas.

Lesson Ten:
Tasting the Bitter

It hurts, a lady said to me at a conference. She said she had an excruciating pain in her knee, and did not know how she hurt it but figured her knee was no longer any good because she was over fifty. I laughed, and she wondered how I could laugh at her pain. I laughed because there was nothing wrong with her knee. She said I did not know what I was talking about. I smiled and said let me rub your knee, I did, and the pain first shifted to her other knee then disappeared. She said, "wow", I then told her, the pain was just something she needed, to pay attention. We talked, laughed and then she went happily along her way.

Pain

What is pain?

Pain is described as a physical suffering or distress due to an injury or illness. Also, the pain of distress or suffering can be mental and emotional not just physical. To understand pain more clearing we must look at pain as an indication that there is something you should take notice and determine, why you are feeling pain. Pain is a warning that something is not in balance and needs your attention. The pain can be minimal or strong according to how important or imperative the situation commands or demands. Normally pain is trying to get you to notice that there is a cause that needs to be addressed before it gets worse or uncontrollable. Most of the time the pain will not disappear until the cause of the pain is addressed sufficiently then the pain can now subside or disappear all together.

Where does pain come from?

Pain is the way a person (whether its in the body or mind) can be notified that there is a challenge. This challenge may also be changed to an opportunity to learn or take action about a situation that needs to be corrected. There is no sickness; there are only challenges and opportunities. Challenges are considered to be a symptom or a problem, an opportunity is being able to heal or correct any problem. When you feel pain it is important to begin to understand what is happening and figure out how to find the cause. In today's society, many people do not sufficiently address their pain, because of the successful advent of a multitude of painkiller medicine on the market. This is great for the pain sufferer, but it can circumvent the learning process and prevent the correction of the cause of the pain. Pain killer medicine masks the pain so that we do not feel the pain, but the pain has not gone anywhere, the cause of the pain is not addressed, but the medication makes us feel good in the process. Many people have discovered that when the pain medication wears off that the challenge still exists, the pain returns and we have to continue to take the pain medication hoping the challenge will correct itself on its own.

To ignore the pain totally, and mask it with medication is not the correct answer for a long-term solution. In the short term, we may feel better without the pain interfering with our immediate performance. This is demonstrated with many athletes who are given medication in order to function at a required competition where they are relied to do well. Sometimes this causes them great sacrifices, but some say the end justifies the means but most who say this do not care about any permanent damage you may suffer as a result of this.

For those who are learning and studying to help others through this pain, realize pain is only an indication that there is something that needs your attention. Modern medicine treats the pain, and in some cases this helps or works well. In other cases, they are unable to correct the problem because the problem may not be simple or a purely physical problem. This requires that those who are spiritual and want to help themselves and others to try first and understand and seek the cause of the pain in order to determine the lesson, the message to the pain sufferer and then effect a permanent healing. This is required so that the student or client will understand and learn valuable lessons in order for the pain and the challenge to not return. Sometimes the pain is light, and because you have ignored it the pain intensifies, then it may become a physical problem that will lead you to take action or end up in the hospital.

What if the pain never leaves or goes away?

If the pain does not go away it is an indication that you have not learned the cause, or the lesson, you are refusing to look and try to seek the answer for what is going on or it is a constant reminder that you must remember or understand the challenge and the lesson or opportunity you are being given.

Be careful

Be careful all pains are not physical, and do not allow anyone to treat your pain by making it worse because they do not understand. The treatment they may prescribe will not correct the problem because it is not the cause. Their treatment may be is evasive and can ultimately cause another (second) or greater challenge, or greater pain. Remember you are in the school of life, and you are constantly learning on a multitude of levels so you must become aware of the challenges and cause of your pain and suffering to alleviate or heal it.

Phantom pain

Phantom pain is when you feel pain physically in a part of the body, but there is actually no trouble or problem in that part of the body. You say to yourself, how could this be? This is easy, and it is something that Healers are confronted with when they try to heal a pain for their client that is actually not there. This is similar to simple explanations such as this little story. I once had a lady as a tenant that I rented an apartment to. This very nice lady every day would complain several times that the apartment was too hot or too cold. Each time I would adjust the thermostat until one day I thought about it and realized that maybe there was not any temperature problem. So I decided to test my theory. Every time the lady would ask me to turn up the temperature I would comply by saying ok. I explained that I would adjust the temperature, and she would thank me, but I would go to the thermostat look at it and then walk away. Then I would wait ten minutes and then call her and ask, "is the temperature ok now", and my tenant would reply, " yes it is fine now". When my tenant would come and ask me to turn the temperature down, I would say ok and then I would repeat the same process by just walking over to the thermostat, look at it, and then walk away. Later I would call the tenant and check to make sure she was ok and would always get the same answer, "it is fine now". Years later, I overheard my tenant explaining to others how I always addressed her requests. I never adjusted the temperature, but I listened to her, and realized there was no actual need to change anything except being sensitive to her requests and needs.

When Healers have, tried to heal a pain in a clients' right side of the body or limb all of a sudden the pain will move to another part of the body and limb. Many times it is a clear indication the pain is not physical and appears to be phantom even though that limb appears to be in pain. The pain appears in the limb or joint, but you can't correct it because it is not actually the cause of the pain, it is just systematic in that region of the body, and will require you to take notice and hopefully search for a cause. Determine what message is being given to you or what is being requested of you to take notice and/or action.

Suffering

What is suffering?

Suffering is defined as undergoing distress, pain, loss, and or injury. This is similar to the Chinese saying "eating the bitter", or the saying "no pain no gain". These are just indications of what suffering is about. Many people suffer many different types of distress, pain, and injuries on a variety of levels. Physical pain can most times be easily diagnosed such as in a broken finger or arm, but other types of pain are not so easily distinguishable such as heartache from a relationship breakup. Suffering sometimes is the result of pain, but pain can be mental or emotional. This type of suffering can be detrimental to health and wellbeing, short, long, temporary, or permanent depending on the lesson.

Suffering can be considered a lesson of varying degrees according to the severity of the lesson that needs to be learned. Temporary suffering is normally a way for a person to learn and move forward, in which the suffering will stop as soon as the lesson is learned or understood. Sometimes suffering is long and arduous, but normally it is not meant to be permanent. This requires some work and understanding to move beyond the particular lesson that a person is learning. When suffering one should continually ask the question, what lesson am I learning or do I need to learn to stop the suffering and move forward to a state of balance or harmony. No one should elect or volunteer to suffer, and if one does it shows a misconception that everyone is here to be happy and not to suffer needlessly after learning valuable lessons, once they are completed.

We have heard many people say to each other that they are here to suffer and "so be it", whether it is a relationship or hardship such as poverty. This is far from the truth, but everyone who has free will can volunteer to suffer, but the suffering can stop when the person has grown to the point of realizing that it is not required. Suffering is only a way to learn whatever one must learn in order to move forward.

Being happy is at the other end of suffering so why are you there where you do not belong? Give up the suffering and move to a place of harmony and happiness by understanding the cause of your suffering. Determine the lesson you are learning or have learned, and then move to a place of healing. Figure out, how to change the challenge into an opportunity to heal, and remove or stop the suffering especially if pain is involved.

Tips, Techniques or Insights

Remember pain is an alert or indicator that there is something you should pay attention. The severity of the pain should be used as a gauge, to understand how important it is to pay attention, and address the problem or challenge, so you can learn and heal it. Some time we have to go through tasting the bitter in order to achieve great things but it should be in training or perseverance of a set goal, not just for suffering sake. Once the lesson is learned the pain will subside. Ask what was the cause and what did I learn and what was the opportunity presented to me.

Be honest with yourself, do not think you are the only one suffering, let go of fear and replace with love. Ask for assistance from those that can discern what is the cause of your pain or suffering. Do not forget the power of meditation and prayer, use the "freedom tool" this tool is the affirmation that you are free from encumbrances from the past, and you have learned your lesson and are free to move forward in a state of harmony, love and Light.

There are a variety of tools to stop suffering. The first is knowledge, the second is meditation, the third is looking in the mirror, fourth is forgiveness (forgive self also), fifth is love yourself, sixth is change your thinking, and seventh is acknowledgement in the "Higher Power" to assist you. Remember the overriding question, "what am I learning and why" and have I learned from this experience sufficiently in order for it to be healed and not repeat itself in the future. Think and be happy. If you feel pain ask in your meditation or your prayers why this pain, what am I learning, and request for this pain to leave you now.

Swadhisthana Second Chakra Strength Chakra

The sacral chakra is primarily considered the sexual energy center

Lesson Eleven:
Health Universe

It is said that Mr. Akins of the "Atkins Diet" became famous by recommending a weight loss solution of eating only protein (mostly meat). This diet was considered revolutionary, and it helped many people lose weight. The only health concern was the increase in cholesterol and excess fat as a result of eating too much meat. The only reason it is essential to understand this is that we must move beyond "one pointed" solutions that solve one problem and cause another at the same time comparable to side effects we receive from some medicines. We must focus on "whole person" solutions instead of just the symptom. For example, many are told they are obese or overweight because they eat too much. This may or may not be the truth in some cases, but it is not the case of all overweight or obese people. There are a multitude of causes why some people cannot burn fat sufficiently, lack good digestion, or have slow metabolisms. Many people starve, suffer and still cannot lose fat because their food intake is not the only reason they cannot lose weight. Some people after major dieting lose needed muscle and eventually become soft and/or fatter so one must be careful.

In order to help many people with their health including our own selves, we must first look at causes that support the entire persons' health. Understanding this we should refocus and gain insight and understanding of a persons' overall health including relationships, food, home, present circumstances, weaknesses, spiritual and emotional state to name a few.

Health vs. Sickness

What is happening in your health universe? Yes, we all have a health universe even if we do not consider this and only think that health is extremely personal, and nobody else's business except when we are supposedly sick and all of a sudden (or we think so) we are sick or wake up in the hospital. Our health universe starts with our internal health (as we can all agree) and then extends outward to our external body and then to our external environment or universe. It is important to understand that our internal and external health affects our universe. So what does all this mean?

Health is important because the ultimate wealth is health, the only thing that money cannot buy. Many people consider health to be external, and it is something for us to experience individually, and something for medical doctors to maintain, but to the initiated it is far from the truth. You maintain your own health, not the doctors or hospitals.

Health

Health is measurable and should be. Society assumes you are maintaining your internal health and you are not just taking your health for granted. As spiritual adepts, (people) we must make sure that we consider our health high on our list of priorities. So what is health? A range of indicators can measure health that include, physical, mental, emotional, psychological, and spiritual to name a few. Starting with the physical we must maintain our bodies. To some we consider our bodies on the spiritual level as our temple in which also includes our minds. The body system is vital, and we should maintain our health and well being as the foundation of our life. What does this mean?

It means we should do our best to maintain our internal systems to stay healthy, and this includes our mentality. This is our charge and maintaining our body systems is first and foremost, which means not waiting until something is wrong hoping all we need to do is take some medication. As spiritual people, we should know "there is no sickness" and if this statement is true then asking the next question is important. Why do we have problems with health or so-called dis-ease or sickness?

The question is it sickness or dis-ease?

Sickness assumes something is wrong, or there is no health. Dis-ease assumes there is something out of balance. In sickness, we have become well and/or un-sick in order to stay healthy as opposed to dis-ease which presumes that there is an out of balance condition that needs to be bought back into equilibrium. When there is an out of balance condition there is still health, and we only need to correct the out of balance condition to return to optimal health. If we rebalance we can be at ease. When we utilize the term dis-ease, we can intellectually understand this is only temporary, and we will be healthy again. Why this so called dis-ease?

Dis-ease

Dis-ease is what many spiritually adept people call a challenge or opportunity. This appearance of dis-ease or out of balance is an indication that something is one of the following:

    A: something is wrong,

    B: something to pay attention to

    C: something to learn or experience

    D: opportunity for growth

This dis-ease is a caused by something that is making our health out of balance, and we must figure out the cause. Many people understand when you say cause and effect but do not know how it is applied to health. In many cases, people do not realize the cause and effect law as it applies to our inner health and the health of our universe. We first ask the question when there is an indication of any dis-ease firstly by "what is the cause?" Second question again we should ask, "what is causing this phenomenon and how do I return myself or my client to balance or ease?"

Firstly we think, what is wrong? Our thinking affects our health, and our thoughts help us to begin to figure out what is happening to us. Thinking is connected to our mentality, and our mentality is connected to our overall health and equilibrium. So you ask your self what is the cause of this dis-ease and then what is the key to get back to a place of ease thereby achieving balance once again ultimately maintaining a state of wellbeing and equilibrium. Once we understand this the importance of maintaining a state of wellbeing is paramount.

Wellbeing

Wellbeing is a state of overall health and wellness that assumes a balance that can be maintained throughout your life. This level of wellbeing also assumes a healthy balance on all levels of our state of being, and this extends from the inside (internal) to the outer external environment that is part of our universe. It is important to understand that the term wellbeing explains our general health on all levels of our internal and external lives and the importance of this extends to our universe. So we should not just focus on the physical body but our entire system that includes the mental and emotional bodies. You have heard the statement "live life more abundantly"; it does not only mean money but also health and wellbeing. This includes our internal and external systems (universe). Do we fully realize that nutrition; exercise, proper relaxation and rest are part of our way of maintaining our wellbeing.

The Inner Universe

How does our inner universe affect the outer universe? Our inner universe is affected by what we think and what we do. What we do affects our overall external universe just as it affects our inner universe. We must take care to insure we all know this and are cognizant of our thoughts and behavior. For example, when we supposedly catch a cold, once catching this cold we consider it to be personal, we do not care about others, so we go to school or work, cough around our family; next we then spread that cold to others thereby causing others to have that cold. We are not considering others or our universe. We do not do anything to protect those around us in our external environment or external universe. Remember we are talking about a simple cold, think about cigarette smoke and consider, what's more, important or imperative. Have you asked the question, how far does this extend into our environment or the universe? Does this bring up a question of what is the universe, what is our universe, should I concern myself or about my universe or should we not take care of our universe in which we are a part? What is happening to our water and air?

The inner universe is connected to what; the answer is of course the outer universe. Some may say the outer universe is not a part of them, but they do not understand, and upon learning how they are connected to the universe, the inner to the external, they can begin to take some ownership of themselves and understand the health and wellbeing of themselves. This extends to close family and extended family as part of the universe, and what we do to maintain our health extends from us and affects our outer universe. Once we know our inner universe, we can understand an outer universe, and begin to change our thinking and expand our minds to see the macrocosm from our inner microcosm. For example, we all drink water and breathe air. Some corporations may not care, but we as people should care.

Outer Universe

The outer universe works exactly the same way. What do I mean by that? What happens in the outer universe appears to have an impact on our inner universe? Consider the zodiac and the entire field of astrology that is devoted to explaining how the outer external universe affects each and every one of us. You have heard the saying, "its in the stars or the phase of the planets, or mercury is in retrograde is the reason you feel like this". If you do not see this have you seen a hurricane, a tornado, and an earthquake? Do these types of phenomenon affect you, yes I would say and those types of phenomenon are dis-eases within the universe that give cause to the universal quest for balance and equilibrium and nature knows how to seek and maintain balance or forge the requirement of moving into balance once it is out of balance if we allow it. Without it, we would not have water to drink, or rain for food, or flowers, or herbs to keep us healthy, and in balance.

What does this do for us, and our lives, our personal universe and the outer universe? This understanding of the universe and how we are connected to it explains the importance of maintaining wellbeing within ourselves. Also, how important it is to maintain the extended universe of which we are a part. Also to see it with eyes that show the interconnectedness of all within the same universe so that we all can be healthy and at ease, and not delegate the unconscious responsibility to others that we assume we are not connected. As healers, we realize the link within to the without and when we try to help those who appear to have a challenge then there is an underlying cause within their inner universe, and it can extend to the outer universe affecting not only their self but others. The ability or success to heal lies within the universe thereby necessitating a universal healing in some cases. It is something to consider within the causation of things.

Tips, Techniques or Insights

Question is how do we maintain our healthy inner universe and outer external universe. One of the ways are to do the constant cleansing, clearing, releasing and letting go of old baggage, clutter, and trash, no longer useful to maintaining a healthy environment. Seeking the cause of any problem and not just the symptom is the way to treat the "whole person". Healing starts with you and your thought. Don't forget to include nutrition; exercise, proper relaxation and rest are part of our way of maintaining our wellbeing.

See health in your life, in you, in your environment and all around you. Your health is important and is part of your wealth. Remove unhealthy situations from around you and maintain your health, breath and your longevity. Remember we all can change for the better. Remember you are not alone! Evaluate your health first then your wellbeing, which includes all facets of your life, emotional, financial, relationships, and your home. Determine what is in balance and out of balance. Begin to bring in balance those parts that are in need. Set a goal toward being in balance, and general wellbeing.

Lesson Twelve:
Letting Go

I met a lovely middle-aged lady at a networking event. I asked why she was not married. She stated "she was jilted at the altar, by some guy who, did not show up. I was taken back thinking how could a guy leave this lovely lady at the altar". She explained that her life was ruined, and she is still hurt from the incident. I wondered why but realized she was ok but still upset. Thinking this happened recently, I asked her when did this happen? She explained that it happened 15 years ago. Shocked I said, "15 years ago" and you are still hurt and angry about it? I told her to "let it go' for she had her whole life in front of her and 15 years were too long to hold a grudge against someone who probably has forgotten all about her. I told her to let it go. Other ladies in the room overheard our conversation, and they also shouted out "let it go".

Letting Go

One of the most powerful tools that will heal you and your universe are called "letting go". At the heart of change is letting go of the past history, things and experiences a person has gone through in their lives. This has major ramifications since we have quite active and extensive memories, which are connected to mental or emotional triggers. In our everyday lives, we actively engage in a host or mired of experiences, positive and negative. Sometimes we let things go, other times we find it difficult to let go and then we carry that experience with us even though the experience may be positive or negative.

So how do we let go and why is it essential that we do? It is called baggage. So what is carrying baggage?

Carrying Old Baggage

Letting go of past experiences or old stuff or old baggage is part and parcel of letting go. The first requirement is to recognize we are carrying stuff that we need and stuff we do not need. This constitutes things we need to let go. Everyone has stuff that we can let go of or need to let go. Most of this comes from the past and sometimes it comes from the present past. For example, we have an argument that makes us upset or a relationship that goes sour. We feel hurt or disappointed, so we move on, but years later we continue to think about those things that happened to us in the past. We remain troubled at the thought of those past experiences even though we have a new relationship, even though the person we argued with is long gone and we have not seen or spoken in years. We first must realize that those past experiences are old and baggage and no longer matters in the present space and time, and we are carrying old baggage. We then can deduce that we need to let go of this old baggage. Once we realize this we can safely let go of old experiences or any baggage that it is time to be released. Other examples of "old baggage" can be old hurts, anger, grievances, grudges, disappointments, negative relationships and other adverse events that have transpired in the past. Why let these things go?

We let these old occurrences or incidents go because the negative situations, and those connected to them including the energy is complete and over. The old stuff will not return unless we draw it by refusing to let go (of the past) and thus by letting go we move forward to the present so we can move forward to the future.

Why is this important?

This is important because you would be surprised, even though many people think they have moved on in situations, events, and/ or relationships surprisingly we have not forgotten the negative experiences that transpired and some mull over these past experiences. Sometimes, we think we have forgotten past actions we have done or have been done against us, and believe we must not let go of the negative incidents that transpired. We say that we have no old grudges or emotions or thoughts of revenge, and this may or may not be accurate. For many times, we are angry or hurt and say things that we regret. We say we are not holding a grudge or vengeful thoughts that appeared to dissipate over time, but all that happens, many times are that we place the incident in the back of our minds. We never let it go totally, and it sits there and sometimes stews and like a mirror reflects in our current situation, life and relationships. We do not understand what is happening, and the problem we experience may not be happening in the present, but we are experiencing a reflection from the past that colors our understanding of what's happening in the present.

You have heard the story from many who state that they keep meeting the same type negative personality in their relationships, and they cannot determine why. The problem may be they are still holding on to some old baggage from a similar old relationship that they have not fully released. One solution is to fully let go of the old relationship, the hurt, the anger, and disappointment and affirm that the past has no influence on the present and whatever transpired in the past is completely finished. You are releasing all of that old baggage, and now you can move forward anew and are fully in the present and the past has no influence on you now!

Cleaning and Clearing

There is an old saying "clean your house". Just as, we clean our house, our cars, our dishes, and do our own spring-cleaning we can also begin to clean our own minds and hearts using the method of releasing through a practice of affirming we are releasing. By the "releasing process" we can begin to clean, and clear old debris from our hearts and minds and begin the healing process. This primarily focuses on the past and present past. As we request release of old clutter we begin to lighten the burden we invisibly carry. Through this, we begin to affirm that we are letting go and are focusing on the present moment, and we will bring vital energy to bear and focus our energy on the present moment instead of past situations.

Past, Present, Future

The past and present have an impact on our future. What we have done in the past, and what we do in the present helps to shape our future. The past positive experiences assist us in the present. The past negative experiences teach us lessons also and after we learn we should let them go. Understanding this in the present we can understand the parable of spilled milk, once we clean it up we should forget about it and not focus on who spilled the milk to hold a grudge. Just let it go and move forward to our bright future. The past, present, and the future appear to be intertwined, but we should focus entirely on the present now because the future is yet to be written and experienced.

Tips, Techniques or Insights

It is important to let old stuff go and remember the present is most important. Stop looking back a wise man once stated, and it is good advice. When you feel there are things that you cannot release ask the question is this something from the present or the past. If it is from the past release it by letting it go by affirming that you are in the present and the past is in its proper place and has no affect on you in the present. Repeat the affirmation until it is gone and has no influence on you.

Just as, it is essential to be present, it is also vital to let go of old stuff that we are mindful or not mindful that ties us to past stuff we need to release. Focusing on past stuff or old baggage is like looking backwards, which will cause interference with our looking forward totally. We must release and let go so that nothing will plague our minds consciously or unconsciously and as we move into the present fully. We can start by cleaning and clearing away the old making way for the new.

Hoarders have a challenge of letting go, cleaning and clearing of old baggage and clutter. Start to clean out some of the old stuff no longer needed from our garage or storage bin; this includes our hearts and minds. De-clutter, let go, do not worry and be happy! Take a walk, imagine as you walk you are exhaling away all of the old stuff, and you are now focused on the present moment in time.

Lesson Thirteen: Missing Pieces

Challenge vs. Opportunity

What and where are the challenges in our lives and where or what are the opportunities. Can you clearly see the challenges before you and does the opportunities present themselves so easily they give you the opportunity to take advantage of them? The answer is only yes or no.

Life continually presents us, with both minor and major challenges. We must deal with these challenges in order to move forward and to resolve, heal, at every juncture in order to solve those things that are required. Why are challenges required? This is a school so we must have fun while we are learning our lessons that we must complete whether we are aware of it or not. There within the challenges are opportunities to learn, experience and grow if we take advantage and look at challenges in a positive manner. A simple challenge is to learn from a mistake we have made in judgment, or learn from a lesson, doing the wrong thing we knew was wrong, but decided anyway to do it. We can take this as an opportunity to learn to do the right thing. To grow we must listen to our own intuition and do the right thing and/or not make premature judgments. This includes doing wrong things others may have us do against our own hearts and conscious.

Opportunities

The challenges though endless, there are also numerous opportunities to learn and grow from where we are. We take a test in school and fail because we did not study, then on the next test we have the opportunity to study and pass the next test with high marks and any other tests in the future. We can have a relationship with a thug type person only to get hit in the head or ripped off then the next relationship we have an opportunity to find a relationship with someone with peaceful demeanor and positive ambitions to have a beautiful, loving and peaceful family if we have learned from the previous me. The challenges and opportunities are endless to help us to grow. The opportunities are the same for us to not only learn, but also to help others to learn, develop and recognize opportunities to assist themselves in their own growth and development.

Teachers come to help those who need assistance and to learn and help others to turn, and one day also helps others. The universe brings many challenges for people to learn how to live and how to help others to see beyond their own challenges. Also, how do you help others to learn from the opportunities that present themselves? One can see a challenge another can see it as an opportunity. For example, what do you see? The challenges also help us to identify those things missing or those things we have not paid enough attention. We can help ourselves by paying attention to what appears to be missing or what we see or know that needs to be addressed.

What is Missing in Your Life?

I went to buy an apple pie, and it smelled just incredible. I knew it would be delicious, but when I got home, opened the box, I noticed that there were a couple of slices missing. Where is the rest of my pie? Should I accept a pie with missing slices? This is a metaphor for understanding what is missing in our own lives. Should we accept that or learn about what's missing and acquire those two slices of critical knowledge?

What is missing or what do you think is missing? Is there anything missing? Perception is important to be able to see challenges as opportunities, and it starts with how you see yourself. Again what do you see is there and what is missing? If we start at what we can see then we can begin to understand what the challenge is versus the opportunity to change what we think needs to change. The challenge; is there anything we can recognize on our own or can learn from some assistance. As soon as we identify what we see or feel that needs to be changed, we can see what is the opportunity that will allow us to fix what it is.

Of course, we will not fix or change that which is not broken, but we will not know until we examine our selves and then determine if we are whole and all is ok in our world. Once we determine all is well in our own lives, then some of us will go beyond and have a higher calling helping others to see their challenges, but cannot see the opportunities without our assistance. Some people see themselves in the mirror of life while others see the world. Some others see all the way to the universe, realizing, they are a part of the universe of which we are all included. They are ready and willing to assist us.

As we ask you what is missing, it may only be your ability to extend your vision to connect to the universe, which, is constantly calling for you to step up and see all of us as one big family, and assist those with limited vision. Our life is filled with many facets and nothing should be missing. Are you aware of what is happening, what you need, what will fulfill you? Are you aware?

Awareness

This is where awareness comes in and is the extension of your gifted vision in order to assist the universe to reach all that may need you and your gift. How aware are we that we can see our own self in the mirror, and then the very same mirror we can see those who need our help and assistance. Our awareness is a gift if we can recognize the challenges as opportunities or the opportunity to help those in need. This can be as a counselor, or coach, or advisor, or healer, to name a few. It is not by mistake you can help others to see through your eyes or heart. Our awareness takes us to the places we can see, and this can include the universe if we only look. At the same time, we must appreciate those who do see their own opportunities and can take advantage of them. Do not negate your ability to recognize opportunities and how to take advantage of them. Also, how do you assist others, because the universe is speaking to you, to help in some small or large way to open your awareness and expand your vision? You do not only live on your block in your neighborhood and community, in your city and state, unless that is all you can see. Challenge yourself and create an opportunity to see more.

Pieces of the Puzzle

As you expand your vision, you will begin to see more and the more. When you can see more pieces of the puzzle you will be able to have the opportunity to view and share with others. Yes, you guessed right life is a puzzle, and the challenge is to get all the pieces in the right places and solve the puzzle. The opportunity is to figure out our your puzzle and then help others to do the same. Now many will say you are on your own, but their vision can only see their own self, and that is ok. There are those who having solved their own puzzles are given the opportunity to help others because they can see beyond their own individual selves, to encompass the worldview and the universe.

Looking at the chart above gives you an understanding to see parts of your puzzle that makes up your life. What is the puzzle, it is called the Tao (pronounced Dao) and what is the end of the puzzle, that is called life in this universe and beyond, live it and help others to live it more abundantly and happy!

Tips, Techniques or Insights

Ask what appears to be missing in your life. Ask what is important that appears to be missing, where is the missing piece(s). Meditate or listen within and first make a list of what you perceive as the missing piece(s). Second ask where are the pieces and ask to be shown where the missing pieces are. Third ask that the missing pieces be given to you so you can be whole. If you receive or perceive nothing is missing give thanks that you are whole and affirm that you are whole, know you are whole. Keep doing this process until you are whole.

Notice the puzzle covers most areas of your life. It doesn't just say work and sleep or play and exercise. It includes all areas of your life as a whole so check all areas and make sure they are all included and addressed. If nothing is missing in your life, and you feel there is a higher calling to reach out, and extend to your community, and world at large, then help them to take advantage of your opportunity to assist them. Realize the universe is reaching out to assist everyone in their challenges and offer opportunities for them to grow and heal.

Imagine you are expanding your vision and awareness. Test and verify that your vision, hearing, etc. is expanding. Check to insure you are gaining expanded awareness of the world and universe. Ask questions about the world and the universe you are seeking answers. Listen within; be aware in your dreams, meditation, and surroundings. Remember a picture is a thousand words. Consider all the pieces in the puzzle; they make up the whole you. Do not buy a pie with slices missing. See yourself whole!

Manipura Third Chakra Solar Plexus Personal Power Chakra

The Solar plexus is connected to our vitality.

Lesson Fourteen:
The Natural Universe

Have you seen a rose lately, or a lily, they are quite beautiful in the spring? The water glistens from the Sun as we view the snow-capped mountains of Himalayas. The redwoods stand so tall majestically against the blue painted sky. I lie beneath a field of golden corn while eating divine wine grapes, from a nearby vineyard stretched across the plains of Napa as nearby hills jump out at me to say Hi. I watch the aquamarine waters of life flow as I view the white sandy beach in the near distance.

Nature

Nature is all around us. Why do we not control nature? That is why it is called nature. This will be hard or easy to understand, but nature is part of that Tao (Dao) that people discuss. What does this all mean? (The Tao is a term used "in Chinese and Asian philosophy" to explain the natural order of the universal way of life. The Tao speaks to the primordial essence or fundamental nature of the universe and all that manifests beyond our control).

Nature is the natural order of things that man does not control or govern by the snap of his fingers or the measure of his whim. I know this will shock some, but this is the natural life that presents itself around us in the universe, and we have no direct control over it. Although there are those who think differently and try to manipulate it to there own benefit. The more we understand this and the less we overly manipulate, the better nature will be able to do what it does without us mucking it up. The nature of things is everywhere in the universe and we witness and observe all that it has to offer and show us on every level. Much of it, we are still learning, and it challenges us every day to learn more if we will listen and not assume we know it all or better than nature does. The universe shows us its limits, unlimitedly and its beauty and power to be and do what it needs to meet its challenges and opportunities every day.

The natural order of things control our lives at the same time so as the universe is ordered so are we to some extent, and we have taken advantage of that as we walk through the natural world and experience the natural universe. So what is next? The next is our ability to experience all we can take in and observe what goes beyond what we think it ought to be. We are prepared for all we see and learn from it. The natural universe is always giving us the opportunity to learn what is, and what is happening at any given time, and how to interact with this nature, and enjoy and experience all it has to offer. This is before we think we are in control and can change the natural order of things that are namely the Tao.

View nature as it is presented then consider how you fit into and interact "within this natural order of things" to see how you perfectly fit within it. Nature has so much to teach us, and experience to expand our view and imagination of what is. Our interaction natural or unnaturally also teaches us many things we will learn, need to know and understand beginning with how to make and deal with change. If change is the only constant than why many things in nature stay the same and some things always change? I can answer this, but you have to utilize your own observations to understand the previous statement, is it true or not? Now we do understand that some say we control nature and change what ever we want to meet our needs and wants. This is where the experience of learning begins, or the Tao speaks to us. We do not control the wind, rain, hurricanes, and earthquakes just to name a few.

Karma

What is karma?

Karma is defined as the reaction to an action. Some call it the law of action versus reaction. Great what does that all mean to us in our lives? It means that as we move and have our being we do things and take action that causes reactions. No cause for concern because this is how we help ourselves to learn and experience the natural order of the universe and all within it. For example, we plant a seed and then the flower grows and blooms. Another example we eat food, and we grow strong and healthy as a child into an adult. This is simplistic, but profound when we begin to understand we grow enough food to feed the entire world, yet we also throw away enough food to feed the world at the same time. So what is the lesson here? We feed ourselves, and we throw away food even though we know there are people who starve every day.

Action/Reaction

The seeds we plant or do not plant provide food to feed the world without bias, but we use food as a commodity and are happy to starve those who cant afford it or do not have access because we think the idea of growing food is only for the fortunate. How karmic is that? It is karmic, only in the sense that our action of refusing to share the food we do not want with those who do not have the money. Since the result is, they starve. We are happy to pay growers not to grow and are oblivious to those who die from starvation.

Kama does affect us in a number of ways because simple things we do show us how the law works, for example, we eat too much and get a sick stomach or we become adversely overweight and blame it on the food. Another example we speed down the highway and cause an accident. We do not perform the required maintenance on our automobile, and it breaks down on the highway twenty miles from home. We meet a person, whom we treat badly in our relationship, and they leave to go with another who treats them better, but we blame them. We worry about every little thing, and 20 years later we get sick and do not understand worrying is no good for our wellbeing and health. We blow up bombs and wonder how come the air and water changes to unhealthy conditions. We shoot all kinds of things in space and then wonder why things drop out of the sky and put holes in peoples' houses. We start wars and wonder why countries do not trust us. We allow pesticides and hormones placed on and in our food and wonder why children get sick. Sometimes we make decisions that are not in our best interest, and when things go wrong we blame others. We go against our own inner urgings and wonder why we do not get the right result.

We spew radioactive materials and carcinogens in the air and wonder why some find it hard to breathe. These are a few examples of actions, and reactions that we witness every day. We can understand karma on a small or large sale but eventually we will have to learn, and understand whether it is in our own life or the life of the planet and universe.

Lessons

The actions we do cause a reaction in our own life and continue into the same within the world and universe. We react to what people say and do and react in a positive or negative way causing a reaction in the same way. Our lives are filled with karmic situations that are learning experiences whether we see this or not, and we also can help others to understand and recognize these situations as we help others in their growth and development. Some say you sow what you reap, whatever that mean or is it "you reap what you sow". There are many lessons, and we want to complete them without causing karma or problems for others if we can.

Sow/Reap

Sow as you reap is the same as action causes a reaction or cause and effect. So what does this mean? Sow as you reap means that whatever you do there is a reaction or an action creates a reaction. This action or sowing dates back to the natural order of what ever you do good or bad, negative or positive, causes a resulting reaction that can be good or bad or positive or negative. For example, you study and go to school and finally you graduate successfully. You treat your employees terrible, and they do poor work causing you to be fired. You plant seeds, and do not water or weed the crop then you receive a bad crop that causes you not to have enough food to feed your family this winter. There are numerous examples, and they are only to help you know what you do that has consequences that can be good or not to your own benefit.

An example is you lie to your friends and family and when you tell the truth no one will believe you when it is necessary. These can be teaching moments just as they are learning moments, and we should understand the concept of teach those who do not know, or are not learning this vital concept. If you are a teacher teach this concept, see how it applies to many and how it will help us to grow and view the health of the earth and the universe. This will begin to help us to graduate fully to understand the Tao of life and the similarities and the opposites. If you are a student learn what you do has an effect (law of cause and effect) on you and others.

In the Land of Opposites

What is similar and what is opposite? Magnets teach us the knowledge of negative and positive, similar and opposite by understanding similar repels and opposites attract. This happens in our universe whether personal or universal we have the concept of opposites everywhere. For example; black/white; light/dark; liquid/gas; lie/truth, sunlight/ moonlight; girl/boy; big/small; open/close; on/off, up/down; in/out; yin/yang to name a few. Understanding these opposites and you begin to see how the Tao (Dao) separates in order to create this universe, as we know it. You cannot change this concept of opposites because they are part of the Tao or the natural order of the universe, but some think they can try only to learn from this concept of why there are opposites.

In order to learn more about the creation of the universe, you must understand the principle of opposites. This can also help you understand why things happen, and it appears that we have no control over nature. Also understanding opposites will teach you about similarities that exist in our universe and within our own selves at the same time.

5 (6) Elements

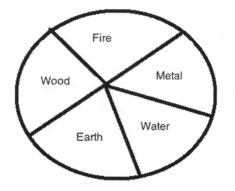

One of things that we must remember is that there is a natural order of things, and the universe is in harmony on many levels. The natural order is focused on harmony, and it includes knowledge of the five (5) elements such as earth, water, fire, metal, wood and ether (sixth). This is critical knowledge to understand how these elements connect to each other and support each other. This understanding will explain the balance, and harmony that exists to keep everything balanced. Chinese traditional medicine understands this perfectly as it pertains to your health. The astonishing importance is that the universal balance is also within you as it is in the universe. Yes, you must also learn how to be balanced within and create inner harmony so you can be well and healthy too. This inner balance is predicated on the interaction with all we do, eat, and deal with in our lives internally and externally.

This balance is well known in Chinese philosophy and shows us how the natural order of the universe created this universe we know and share. There is a symbiotic relationship within these elements which shares its relationships such as without fire there would be no metal, but without air, there would be no fire, without earth there would be no wood, earth supports water, and without ether there would be no universe for us to explore. This natural phenomenon is part and parcel of nature, and we experience it within our own lives. The same elements are within us, and we must also be balanced. When we eat properly, drink sufficient water, get our nutrients, and rest our internal systems function properly, and we are balanced.

Tips, Techniques or Insights

Spend time in nature to see what you can learn. Learn to see what nature is telling you, teaching you, trying to share with you. Think and meditate about the natural order of things. Think about how to create balance in your life. Think and meditate on karma. Are you creating karma negative or positive? Ask are you in karmic situations and why. What are you learning from it? (Remember karmic situations can be positive or negative so do not assume its not good). You can get rid of any bad karma, so meditate or pray to clear any karma you do not need. Seek the advice of a qualified Spiritual Teacher or advisor to assist you. Some people come and go in your life due to karma.

Remember the law of action/reaction means that, for every action, there is a reaction and doing good creates good reactions and responses most of the time. Doing bad things can bring a similar reaction or consequences. If there are things in the past, you did that were not so good do not beat yourself up, first forgive yourself and then forgive others. Think only good thoughts release any bad thoughts. Why? Thinking good thoughts also create good outcomes. Remember thoughts are things. You can change your thoughts.

Also, the philosophy of the 5 elements is to understand being balanced and healthy. It is important so ask yourself, are you in balance? If you sense you are ok, then great. If you sense you are not try to sense or meditate on which element is out of balance and focus and see that element is bought into balance with the other elements to begin to rebalance yourself. From time to time check and determine that you are in balance especially if you feel out of kilter. Think do good things and get good results. To understand the five elements learn how they are connected to the body organs and the universe. To assist you, a table is added below.

Five Element Universal Chart (Zangfu Organs)

Element	Organs (Zang)	Organs (Fu)	Time of Year	Direction	Color
Wood	liver	Gall bladder	spring	east	green
Water	kidneys	bladder	winter	north	black
Fire	heart	Small intestine/ triple burner/pericardium	summer	south	red
Metal	lungs	Large intestine	fall	west	white
Earth	spleen	stomach	center	Up and down	yellow
Ether				universal	

Lesson Fifteen:
Learning from the Universe

You thought that when you finished high school or college that the lessons or learning was over. Well that is the furthest from the truth. Life is a school, and like school there is much to learn, classes to pass, and you can earn degrees. Life can give you a master's degree or teach you many lessons.

Understanding Life's Lessons

Many people do not realize that life is a lesson entwined within many lessons. There are many tests and many opportunities to learn and pass all the tests. Learn what we need to know and move on through life successfully. Like school we will pass our lessons and some we will have to repeat and some we may think we fail only to retake and pass successfully. All have opportunities to learn and pass their lessons successfully if they try and want to but it does take some work, study, and learning on the go or what some of us lovely call OJT (on the job training). There are those who quote that we are not given more than we can handle, but I like to use the idea that there are helpers and teachers around that will help you become successful and assist you to pass your test and lessons. Unlike school, they cannot take your test for you, but they can help and tutor you to be able to gain what you need to know and help decipher what you have learned or need to know in order to take advantage of your lessons.

It is imperative to learn our lessons so that we can move forward without having to retake the same old lessons. The problem is sometimes we do not know what the lessons are until we are met with tests. These tests help us to gain insight to situations and events that transpire expectantly or un-expectantly. After we learn our lessons, we may have to learn other lessons that are not about us but about helping others to learn and pass their own tests.

Yes, there are students, student teachers and teachers, which one is you?

Why are you here, to learn or to teach or a combination of both? The universe is calling some of you to learn more and do more, teach and help others to learn. Are you willing to learn, teach and be who you are to become. This requires us to change our thinking as to why we are here, to go beyond the idea of "party until the wheels fall off " mentality unless that is why you are here. For those who are not clear then they should meditate or seek advice as to why they are here, what lessons they need to complete and insight into what lessons they have passed, failed or have not taken so they can complete as much as they can in the near future.

Change as a Paradigm

Change as a paradigm is for changing your thoughts before "the wheels fall off" and help you to focus on accomplishing what you need to do to move forward, knowing you have completed this school and are ready to move forward. Change is difficult for some and for some that is their lesson. It requires you to change your thinking or help others to change their thinking in order to learn and understand all the knowledge they are gaining. Part of the lesson here is to transform your thinking or learn from your thoughts or confirm your thinking is righteous. It is difficult to say what is right or wrong, but there is the law of consequences or karma that teaches us to understand decisions we make, and the opportunity to make positive change for positive results. We must always look at change or things remaining the same, what is right or wrong is only what we perceive or know from the insight we gain and lessons we learn like touching the hot stove once, to know it is too hot to touch again.

The importance of this is also to know we all learn at different speeds, so some are slow and some learn fast, but we all will learn sooner or later. This is important when trying to understand your own lessons while assisting others learning their own lessons. With no judgment, we are able to help those who need our assistance and guidance in order to complete their lessons successfully. So changing your thinking is required to learn and know more.

Tips, Techniques or Insights

First remember change is the only constant in the universe. This means everything is changing on some level whether perceived or not. Everyday many changes occur, just as, we think much remains the same. You can discern the changes in you. Some things are important, and you should from time to time perceive changes required within you. Meditation will help you in discovering changes within you. Seek advice if you need help.

Then there are the voluntary changes that we implement for our own life. There is the opportunity to change what we do not like or feel is not right in order to make change happen. Ask yourself what is it you need to change, if nothing great, if something then make changes knowing this is the best for you. If you are a teacher or coach help others to focus on what changes they need to make, for their own highest good. This requires an ability to not be judgmental or biased while helping others to succeed, and be the best they can be. We are all in different places, going in a multitude of apparent or not so clear directions, but we are all in the same universe. Do our best is why we change or help others to change for the best. Change those things that are for the best. Do not complain about why things are not changing. Change whatever you need to that is essential and know you can change. Remember, some things we cannot change that we do not control, but I can control myself.

Lesson Sixteen:
The Working Universe

Brock is an investment banker, Tom is a doctor, Sam is an engineer, while Jill is an attorney, and Joe is a landscaper, Marie is a secretary, Bob is a plumber, and Jane is an elementary school teacher. Moe is a bricklayer and Sylvia cleans houses. Lana is a body worker, Geo is a life coach and Helen teaches Yoga. What do all of these people have in common, they are all workers, and they work!

Work

Work is something we all can identify with because we all do it, are involved in it in some way shape or form. Do you work? What kind of work do you do? There are all types of work. We consider working into three categories such as physical work, work for financial reasons, and artistic work. There is a fourth type of work we call higher or spiritual work, sometimes also called benevolent work.

This work is for those who are considered "light-workers" or those who do work that is spiritually motivated and is done to benefit mankind and the greater universe which includes all of us. This work is important, and it helps to raise the consciousness of individuals, communities and the planet. It differs from physical work that we do every day in our homes and around us locally including exercise for our bodies. At the same time, its different than doing business that is for financial reasons only while important is typically done to benefit the individual and his family. It directly provides monetary results for the individual and their own benefits. The work that includes

93

benevolent work is utilized to help people and also help those who are doing this work. It can be for those other than the individual, but it has a two-fold purpose, and it can be for wellbeing. For example, some people give to charity to use as a tax write off. Some people create charities but never give any or very little of the donations to the cause they are for whom they are collecting. Some dedicate their lives to helping others, this we call higher work.

Higher Work

Higher work or Spiritual work, on the other hand, is mostly for the help and healing and is done to help those involved and all who are connected to it, examples such as healing the earth, teaching people to heal others, helping others to grow and etc. This work can be done with the full knowledge of all involved or can be totally invisible to those benefiting this work but done to help all. Many are involved in spiritual work whether known consciously or unconsciously. If you are called to do this higher work you are helping all selflessly and are working "with the universe" to help all. Many are called to do this work to help the universe and, so know you are helping all on a universal level. Some are just now being called to make the decision to work on a universal level so when you get the call do not hesitate, help us to uplift your community and create a better world while working with the universe.

Failure versus Success

Failure is a problem that many deal with and it has created stress in the life of many people. Failure is or may be on the road to success, or maybe there is not any such thing as failure. Maybe it is just a stone on the road to success and is just there for us to pass by on our way to success. We should know that success is straight ahead, and we should not worry or be afraid of anything designated as failure. That is a judgment that most times is evaluated on the basis of individual preconceived notions of what appears to be a success or failure. What we think is a success or failure, should be determined by ourselves, knowing that we have a choice on how to make that determination by our own criteria. Some say you opened a store for three years and broke even or loss money but to the discerned eye the fact you opened the store, and it lasted three years is a resounding success. The fact you did not make the money does not make you a failure. The fact that you learned to swim but did not win a gold medal makes you a success that you now can swim well. Others outside may assume by their rules that you are a failure, but you are not supposed to determine your life by some other person's judgment and criteria. We have to caution ourselves when you listen to others with their opinions or judgments that affect you and your self-esteem, or what they consider failure and success. This is important when we decide what we need to do or not do to be a success in life. Living is a success. Other things we do are subject to our own judgment and should not pay attention to others.

No one can say whether you were successful or failed in life because that is a judgment. No one can say who is or who is not doing what they may succeed at but we can help all to be successful with what they are trying to accomplish by providing objective insight, information or assistance. We should help others to do and be the best they can be, and then get out the way for them to go do their best. Our job as light workers is to assist others in being their own success and accomplishing their goals!

Life's Goals

Life brings us a multitude of goals. Some of these are easy to accomplish, and some are difficult. Some goals require our own sense of decision making to decide what we should accomplish or not. What we should do or not do is up to whom? What is worthwhile or not, and which goals are paramount and vital to what we would like to complete in our own lifetime? What goals should one choose in this life? Whose life is it comes to mind. It is not difficult to determine this, but we can all start with it in our own life and know we can make our own decisions. As a child, many decisions are made for us hopefully in our own best interest. Most times we have no control of that portion, but when we reach adult hood we can begin to make decisions that are in one's own best interest. We can begin to fulfill goals we have set that we personally would like to complete.

Goals are projects, one envisions or decides that we want to complete. It requires us to continue to make many decisions, and complete tasks to achieve those goals. You should write down goals broken down into two lists, one short-term goal, and one long-term goal. The short-term goals should be completed within one month to one year and the long-term goals can take 3 to 5 years. These goals can change over time so it is important to review your list to determine those goals completed and those goals still relevant or have to change. Keep your list private but make sure you review it from time to time.

Who should be making the decisions?

You should be making your own decisions but can seek advice, but remember it is your goal. Too many times, the biggest complaint I hear from clients are that the goals and decisions they have made in their lives is not their own. They do not like the decisions but do them anyway and feel forced and controlled, complaining they are not living their own lives. Many of these clients are successful but are not satisfied. I acknowledge it is important to make and set goals /decisions, but it is also important to be happy with those goals/ decisions, especially if the goals and decisions are connected to your own personal happiness, self esteem and success. You can change any goal you deem no longer useful. As they say, it is your life anyway.

Tips, Techniques or Insights

There are all types of work. Are you working, if not think about what work you need to do, want to do? If you are working think about how you are doing, and if you need to prepare to do more or whether you are doing what you love, and/or do you need to study to learn more. Are you doing what you want to do, or do you feel what you are currently doing, is your life's work? If your work is serving mankind or want to are you working to make that dream come true? If not think about how to be of service to mankind. Also, are you serving yourself too because you cannot forget you deserve too, do not leave you behind. Remember others do not determine your success. If you get or got knocked down get back up. You determine success or failure. Failure can turn into success. Let go of what's not working and keep doing what's working. Set realistic goals and do not be afraid to change goals if necessary. The "ride or die" thinking is great but not feasible for the long term. If you have to, you can always change goals.

There are goals that appear to be made for us to use our special gifts. These gifts are part and parcel of what makes us happy in the end. If you are not happy with a goal remember you can change that goal and/or decision. if we choose a wrong goal or make a wrong choice we can change that decision also. We should be happy with our decisions and goals but also know we can change any or all that we do not want or love at any time. This is not stressed enough to many people who are extremely disappointed. Many of us come with specific goals and decisions made for us, but those are macro decisions and goals, and we still will make the micro decisions within our everyday lives. Those high-level decisions and goals we had also agreed to before we arrived here, we are destined to complete them knowing or un-knowingly. If you are not sure what you need to complete, seek advice and review your list, if you want to know why you're here and what you here to do meditate on it or visit a spiritual teacher or mentor.

Lesson Seventeen:
Beyond Self

Have you heard the story of the old man, retired, successful, walking on the beach alone, stating to himself on how he struggled, suffered, and finally made it, becoming a success? As he is walking, he is making footprints in the sand, but as he turns back toward his beach house he sees another set of footprints next to his. He looks around and sees no one else. As he looks at the two sets of footprints, shocked he says, "oh so now you (God) come to share in my success, you were not around when I was struggling then there was only my set of footprints". A voice rang out and said "those footprints were not yours they were mine, during those years you were struggling I carried you".

Being Alone or Never Alone

As we begin to meditate and contemplate ourselves, and the universe we realize much about ourselves and then we begin to move beyond ourselves but before that we question, "am I by myself". Many people feel alone like the whole world has disappeared, and we are left to fend for ourselves not understanding how we got here. Some of us then take credit for all we have accomplished or done or not have accomplished. Either we accept credit or pass blame to confidently state we are alone. Of course, this is because we are not fully, comprehending that we are part of that universal which means, "are we truly alone" or are we just thinking we are or were alone. For this then we must pull back and ask this delicate question are we alone? To think you are alone means you do not understand how the universe works.

Contemplating

I think that I am, I think I am all that I am, I think and know I am, all has been said. Think is the answer, listen is crucial, light is the way, mind is available, spirit is happy to show the light of the way, the importance is to see and hear. It is imperative to go beyond your own individual thoughts and mind to the universal and contemplate the universe, the one within the all, and how we all become one. This will lead us to the Universal Mind. So we should contemplate the Universal Mind to understand that, which is beyond our reach to understand and raise our consciousness to the higher level.

Realization

Do you recognize whom you are, why you are here? Do you want to know? I realize that some people think it is better not to be aware or just unconscious. There is some confusion and a need for clarity in the world so you must choose what is beneficial to you. We realize all that is in front of us but even then many choose to ignore all of this. As spiritual people, you must first understand whom you are then realize you are on a spiritual path that requires you to know why you are here realizing you have much to remember and accomplish. This will require you to do some inner work to be able to successfully gain the knowledge you seek in order to know about you, others and how that connects you to the universal. It is the act of remembering whom you are now and what you need to accomplish that will make you realize what you need to know about the world, and the universe. Also, it will help you in knowing why you are here and help you to achieve all your goals. You must understand how you fit and are connected to the universe in order to understand your connection to all who exist in this current universe.

Realize you must learn how the universe is communicating with you, and that it is time for you to get busy learning all you need to know. You then can realize the work you have to complete, along side of the work that needs to be done to help others. Who may appear to be asleep or unconscious to what is happening around them. This is important because as you achieve you then can turn and help others to achieve.

Tips, Techniques or Insights

What do you realize about your community, your state, country, the world and further the universe? What do you realize about your connection to other people, the world and the universe? What new have you discovered when you contemplated others, the world, the Universal Mind. Spend some time meditating, and contemplating about all in the universe, the circle of life, and why you are not alone. Understand how we are connected together. We should discover more about the world and its people. Most are spiritual and are on a similar path whether they or you know it or not. Do not assume or prejudge without knowing the facts or truth. We achieve successful goals and produce excellent work if we realize we are not alone, and we are part of the Light of the universe.

You may climb the mountain and think it is over, but when you turn to look up there is another higher mountain to climb, including helping others traveling on a similar path. There are many levels to reach, much to understand, many goals. The goal is the path, and the journey is the way and the way is in front of you.

Ajna Brow Chakra Sixth Chakra

The brow chakra that auric hues and other visual
images are intuited clairvoyantly.

Lesson Eighteen:
Knowing

A guy once asked his friend if what he knew about a subject was correct, his friend answered, "I'm 99.5 % sure", and with that he said to his friend, "you actually do not know". If you say you know for sure 100% then you know and are not guessing. We do desire to know.

What Do You Know

We think many thoughts. We assume sometimes that we know, and we guess a lot or listen to others whom we believe or take for granted that they know. Many times we find out later they were wrong. Of course, we all need to ask questions and want the answers, but we also have a need to know the truth and what is correct. The question is what do I need to know, and who truly knows what I need to know? To know is crucial because If you ever read a book on any subject, you will find that there are several books on the same subject, that may contradict each other such as, for example, what does a certain color means or represents. I have heard many people say they know because they only read it somewhere or saw it on TV. That is not enough.

Do they actually know? Can we say for sure or do we only know when we know our own self for sure? So how do we know? I can say the stove is hot but can I say that when someone tells me the stove is hot or do I need to touch it to know and confirm it is hot, when I actually touch it. I would answer that you will know when you are close to it and feel the heat or if someone credible tells me its hot. I can choose to take their word or lastly I can touch it and will know in an instant.

(You do not have to get burned to know the stove is hot). This does not mean you have to touch everything; a sense (gift) of knowing is best. To know all is and known and knowledge is universal.

Knowing

Spiritually we have to trust that we know, and cannot guess or assume, especially when we share information, insight or perceived knowledge with others, who may presume that we know what we are imparting. At the same time, we will want to share and teach others to speak from a place of knowing and hope that we are representing ourselves correctly from that place of knowing.

So how do we know? We have to rely on the gifts that give us the capability of knowing we know. These gifts come from some of the basic gifts we already have. We can see, feel, hear and utilizing additional gifts or talents we can know. We can move beyond our own cognitive abilities and utilize gifts that allow us additional insight, and knowledge that others do not have to discern more. Part of knowing relies us to confirm and verify what we know before we can assure others that we know what we are talking about. This will require us to communicate what we know is true and not guess or just rely on others, or, what we have read in some books especially when imparting exceedingly vital information. If you do not know it is best to say I do not know when imparting vital knowledge to others who will use this information in crucial situations. We can draw wisdom from those who have knowledge. Do you know the past, present or future?

All is, and nothing is, they say. There is a lot to know, and a lot to know in the universe, but that only pushes us to understand and learn more. Many things are there in front of us and very easy to learn and understand, there are others things that have to be discerned using others gifts and skills that are not apparent to some but available to those who can see or hear or feel or intuit what others cannot. These gifts are to help us in finding other information not readily available to others. Once we gain information we can use that knowledge to help others who want to know this expanded knowledge.

What does this all mean? It means you have a need to know, but what do I need to know? Firstly you need to know all about you. Yes, you do come first because you need to know you before you begin to know others. First go within to learn and know whom you are! Knowledge is key and knowing you is a minimum requirement. Knowing comes from a place of Divine Knowing and Truth. Once you know you the next step is learning to understand your environment until you know the universe. Once we learn and know we can learn to impart knowledge to others, and we will reach a state of knowing we know. This is not to be taken lightly, but it is a gift and must be treated as such especially when we use it to share and help others. Before we impart what we know though we need to understand what we know and what we learn so that we can justify ourselves to others. Knowing what we know is one thing, understanding what we know in order to explain it clearly to others is another thing.

Understanding

Most importantly when we know we also must understand what we know. This is the next step called understanding what you know. This is imperative because many may know but when asked to explain what they know sometimes find it difficult to explain in a clear succinct way. To know what we are sharing, saying and imparting to others is crucial because it will affect others. Can we explain, what, why, when and how when questioned as to what we know and the extent of what we appear to know and get people clearly to understand us without any confusion? This is a tall order, but it is for us, and indispensable when helping others to be clear. When you are dealing with yourself (knowledge) and others, you must question or ask and answer the question until you are clear and are receiving all you need to know in order to understand clearly what you know. This may include the continuation of questioning until you have received all the information you need to fulfill your knowledge on a given subject.

For example, when healing others and yourself, you must know and understand the cause and healing to insure there is no repeat of the same incident or challenge in the future.

Tips, Techniques or Insights

Ask yourself what do you know for sure, and what don't you know. What do you realize you need to know and learn now? Meditate on what else you need to know? Ask yourself do you understand what you know. Do you want to understand more? If you need clarification, ask for it. Begin to learn or discern what else you need to know and understand. Seek advice, awareness and ask questions until you learn all you need to know. Do you ask questions and expect an answer? Go within to receive the answers and know you are receiving the correct answer. If you do not understand, ask for clarification. If you can see then know a picture is a thousand words including dreams. If you still do not understand then seek an experienced spiritual advisor. We must grow, connect to the universal and come from a state of knowing which is a gift from the Higher Source. We should ask for wisdom, but we also should ask for understanding!

Anahata Fourth Chakra Heart Chakra

The throat chakra is our voice center. It is through our
spoken word that we express our truth to others.

Lesson Nineteen:
The Heart of the Universe

What is in your heart, love or other things that do not belong? Jill and I had an excellent relationship, and we were close, but I noticed at certain times she would get upset for no reason. I knew it was not I because it happened several times for no reason. One time when we were preparing dinner, all of a sudden she got angry for no reason and started to holler at me. I explained to her not to take out her personal problems on me. I then enquired as to why she would get upset at different times for no apparent reason. She stated that she cared about me, but from time to time she would think about the old relationships in her heart. Those relationships were no good, and they made her angry when she thought about them. I told her to take a look in her heart for love, and let the bitter memories go out, so they would not interfere with her present relationship.

The Heart

What is the heart of the matter? The answer is, the heart is the home, and where the seat of love lies. The heart beats for you and keeps you alive, which is one of its primary functions but the other is to show you the way. The way is through the heart because love is whom we are, and the flow of love is "in the heart" to touch us, and those whom we give love. The heart represents the fifth chakra, and it is essential to see love in the heart. We should learn all we can about the heart and love.

Love

One of the definitions of love is defined as a, "profound tender", affection toward another person. Another definition is a deep affection or attachment to someone else, and another is a sexual passion or desire. The cause of different definitions speaks to the fact there are different types or examples of love. Firstly the love of self is vital and should be stressed to all that you must love your self first before you love anyone else. Secondly love for our family and children are another type of love that we should learn to recognize as special. Thirdly love for friends and relationships is another whether they come and go, touch our lives for a reason, or stay forever. Love is an attraction that flows from us to others and visa versa.

Children are conceived through love, from our hearts and are there forever; no matter what you hear people say. Some people think and feel love is "like a poker chip" to give to whom we feel like and to take away when we feel like it or sell to the highest bidder, but love is more sacred than that. Some believe the heart is yours, and you can do what you want with it, but that is from a lack of knowledge and understanding. The lack of understanding is the concept of love being given, held from, taken away, sold, or closed to all. The heart is not supposed to be an emotional tool that we can use as a bargaining chip. We should not take the heart hostage or be used or abused by those who take advantage of those with open hearts. With this said some like to allow love to be pushed aside and hate to fill up space in the heart to prove that they have control of love. It also does not mean because you love you should become a doormat, whipping post or a slave to prove it.

Hate

Hate is defined as an intense dislike or aversion toward someone or something. This intense dislike brings negative energy to the heart, and it is wrong because it does not belong in the heart or around you for you are conceived and supposed to be surrounded in love. Hate is and should be dismissed from your heart so your heart can freely love yourself and others. Releasing hate is to let go of past stuff that we dislike so we can do what we like. Old stuff we hate in terms of things that happened in the past should be let go, and much learned from it. We should reject negativity from our lives to focus on things, and others we love in our lives, without the excess baggage of old stuff that we dislike intensely, and gets in our way of freely loving. Then we can appreciate the love we have for our own self, family and others. Allow our love to blossom and feel or see the love flowing to and from our hearts when our loved ones are around us.

Selfish Love

The question then comes up should we keep all our love just for ourselves and then anyone else can barter for our love or do we just keep it locked in our heart box, and no one can get any unless they kowtow or bow to our will and personal requests. Or do we dole it out like a small mint to all who share their love with us. Selfish love is good for you because it is best when we love ourselves first and then others such as loved ones and family. Some people think their love is only for themselves, and it is so precious they are not giving up any no matter what. There are those who feel also that love is only for close family including myself, and do not have to share any of this love with anyone else. This is ok because you are sharing love and loving yourself. There are those who have a lot of love for not only their own self but also share it with loved ones and those in need. There are those who give love but get nothing in return this is not suitable, you should be receiving love in return.

Tips, Techniques or Insights

Ask yourself first where is your heart. Second is your heart open. Do you give and receive love? Do you share? Are you hating, you or anyone else? If so begin to release any and all hate (that include grudges). Surround yourself with love. Release any hatred toward anyone else and affirm you no longer hate or begrudge anyone (can say the name(s) and forgive yourself and affirm you have no animosity toward anyone in any past or existing relationship. Remember love and hate cannot live in the same place. Do not give up your energy to hate. Do not teach your children to hate, teach them love.

Ask are you selfish, do you give, are you open to receive. If not begin to learn to share, if you give love be open to receive love too that is the balance. Give without expecting something in return. Giving advice is giving also it does not have to be only money.

It is essential to learn that love and hate do not belong in the same place. It is like putting negative energy into the same bowl that you put positive energy, and wonder why you do not feel the love potential of your heart. The heart is a place of love, and there should be no hate or fear in it is place. Remember love yourself first.

Lesson Twenty:
Beyond the Selfish Universe

Selfless Love

This is where the selfish lovers separate from the selfless lovers who show love to and for others without them having to ask for it. This happens when we live our lives thinking and feeling that we have love not only for self and family but also for those who are in need of love. Many, who step forward and show love, and give without worrying about what they are getting, in return, see this kind of love throughout their lives. Selfless love is not selfless if you are expecting to get something in return, that is selfish love. So it is essential that we know the difference and not get confused. Today many are finally realizing the imperative to be selfless lovers and help those less fortunate or to care about the earth and what is happening to mankind, the animal kingdoms, and the universe. This will help to bring us to the level of people realizing it does not cost to show and give love. We also learn it is ok to receive love from those who give it unselfishly to help us to be the best we can be. Love is not just about money. Love is precious, and you should know you deserve to receive. Let's do not get it confused with sex either. Selfless love is about caring and sharing with others to help them without expecting some reward in return.

Compassion

As the world changes and people grow to understand this is one planet, one universe of which we are all a part and have a need to share its wealth, beauty and protect it for all to enjoy. This special level is one of compassion, it is the higher form of love because it comes from those who understand that we are all one and a member of the same world and the universe, no matter any manmade choices or lack of understanding for mankind. Compassion is also a gift.

Are you compassionate? Can you love everybody? Do you love all? Do you love all no matter their race, religion, and creed? Do you wish all to be the best they can be? Do you think we should all share in the goodness and at the same time, we should protect the downtrodden, the so-called weak, defenseless? Can we protect the suffering from the powerful that blow up the dreams of others, so they can be richer, and more powerful? If so you are showing compassion that is needed to insure we all can be whom we are meant to be and that we all share love by giving and receiving love. Compassion is a gift that we share with others. It is also one of the six perfections because we all should strive to maintain a compassionate heart. Compassion can be attained if you wish to give love unconditionally to others without expecting anything in return. This includes doing things for people and all mankind, the earth and the universe.

Tips, Techniques or Insights

Look for evidence of compassion in nature, it is there if you will look. Compassion is crucial for all, the birds, the bees, the fish, the people, the Earth, all within the universe. This is not as easy as it sounds, but it is doable when we give up the idea that our love is just for us and realize our hearts can send and receive love to and from all who also unselfishly love and want all to receive love. Giving love without a thought of getting and sharing what you can is signs of compassion. Helping others is a sign of compassion when the heart is in the right place.

YIN YANG SYMBOL

Lesson Twenty-first:
Healing the Universe

Energy

Once we understand love in the world we should learn and know about energy. Energy is everywhere in the universe and is essential to all life. What is life? Life is considered to be those organic mechanisms that are distinguished from inorganic mechanisms that do not appear to exhibit growth, and reproductive functions that create universal life. Many consider life to be activity, but many adept and knowledgeable people consider life to be about energy.

Energy is called by many names such as breath, Prana, Chi, Ki, life force and love. No matter the name, life is called energy, and without energy there is not any life. There is subtle energy considered love to gross energy such as a rock. Everything is imbued within an energy field (if it is alive) no matter how fine or gross, slow or fast, thin or dense. Energy flow is what keeps us moving ever forward and is shared by all in existence such as the breath we all share and experience. The sun exhibits a high-energy source and helps plants to grow that feed the entire planet. The movement of water creates energetic flow (electricity) that can power a building and light up the world.

When considering people energy flows within and makes us healthy and keeps us alive. Our bodies are supplied with energy from the universe, breath, food, energy from the earth, from the sun and plants. Love is an energy source that we use when we share love with love ones and others whether we realize it or not. Energy helps to keep us healthy and heals us when we feel we are weak or appear to be sick. The body has different types of energy called yin or yang (masculine or feminine or hard or soft, hot or cool) that is in balance when we are healthy. When we heal ourselves, energy is a part. When we heal others we utilize healing energies to accomplish that task in many cases. The energy we receive from plants and the air is essential and must be treasured the same as the internal within our bodies. Energy also comes from food. It is part of the temporary energy that powers the body

Yin Yang Energy

Yin energy is soft, cool feminine earth energy; yang energy is a hard, warm masculine universal energy. Men are yang with a touch of yin and women are yin with a touch of yang. This is the perfect balance to keep men and women healthy. Nature shows these same energies in balance and men and women are balanced within nature. This is also reflected by the Chinese yin yang symbol. Earth energy is yin, sun and energy from above is yang energy. Yin and yang healing energies are part of our internal systems and connects us to the earth and universe.

Healing

Healing who, what, when you, me, all of us. Can we? If there is no sickness then what is right and what is wrong? Healing is the solution. Sickness is an appearance that challenges us to seize the opportunity to learn, heal and grow if we choose. Can we heal? Yes, we can and we always have an opportunity to heal, and grow.

As we sense or feel things are not quite correct we need to heal those situations whether it is on the physical, mental, or energetic levels. Healing is vital in order to correct imbalances. Healing helps us recognize those things we need to address and learn and correct so that we can move forward or grow. For example, we exhibit hate issues from the past but the problem keeps popping up in the present. We have to let go of that anger and hatred, so our hearts are only filled with love so we can have successful relationships going forward in the future. So we can heal situations that make us angry by releasing that anger and hate and filling that space in our heart with love.

Self-healing is essential because you must know how to heal yourself. For example, you had some feelings of weakness but cannot find the source of the problem because the answer is not drinking more "Red Bull" or other energy drinks. Under proper intuitive scrutiny, you find out you are suffering from stress and worry. The perfect solution is to learn to heal you by releasing that worry and stress. Upon accomplishing that task and learning not to worry or create internal tension, you find out that now you have ample energy and can learn also how to build energy.

Longevity

Longevity is also connected to energy. There are many reasons why people live to a ripe old age of 125 years. They have abundant energy. They know how to receive energy and preserve their energy. There are ways to build and increase energy, and conserve energy. You can start to do things such as sleep properly, eat proper foods, exercise, relax, do not worry or over stress to name a few and know that the universe is full of boundless energy. There are exercises that focus on longevity such as yoga, tai chi and Qigong to name a few.

Tips, Techniques or Insights

Learn more about energy. Learn more about the energy that flows through us, and the earth, all the way to the universe. Energy is everywhere in the universe, learn to discern that universal energy. Learn how energy can heal you.

Love plays a role and helps us to heal others as energy flows, and love flows throughout the universe. When we share unconditional love, it also helps us heal others and ourselves. You must learn how to gather and build the chi energy from the universe to assist you in self-healing and then the ability to heal others.

There is a multitude of examples of self-healing or assisted healing from gifted healers who can assist you in your self-healing. This ability to heal oneself is only a step to be able to help others to heal themselves. The importance is to be able to utilize your gifts to help others heal and grow even as you heal yourself. If you are a healer or light worker heal you first then learn to help and heal others. Take a course and meditate on how you can use your healing gift and abilities to help others. Learn about longevity and practice it.

Lesson twenty-two: Cultivating the Chakras and the Energetic Universe

Chakras and their Meanings

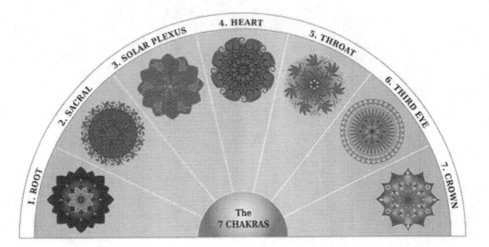

Chakras

Chakras are energy centers contained within the energetic system of all individuals. These energetic centers when properly opened and functionally help us to be an optimum state of wellbeing and health. These chakras also connect us to the universal energies that flow from the earth to the universe.

Chakras should be tested to insure they are functionally correctly and if not then be healed so that we can take advantage of the energy, wisdom and healing they bring us.

Chakra One: Muladhara

Location: Base of Spine

Color: Red

The root chakra is the grounding force that allows us to connect to the earth energies and empower us. We heal through earth's energy flowing up through us.

Chakra Two: Swadhisthana

Location: Lower Abdomen

Color: Orange

The sacral chakra helps maintain a healthy yin-yang balance. Although the sacral chakra is primarily considered the sexual energy center, it is also the center where individual creativity resides.

Third Chakra: Manipura

Location: Naval

Color: Yellow

The solar plexus chakra defines our self-esteem, our personality. We are alive, and active, we eat and extract the energy from food.

Fourth Chakra: Anahata

Location: Heart

Color: Green or Pink

The heart chakra is considered to be the love center. This chakra houses also heartbreak, grief, pain, and fear, are all emotions that are felt intensely within this energy vortex. Learning self-love is a powerful initiative to insure and maintain a healthy heart chakra. Pink represents unconditional love. We turn green with love of self and family, those close to our hearts. We turn pink when expanding our love unconditionally to others and the universe.

Fifth Chakra: Vishuddha

Location: Throat

Color: Sky Blue

The throat chakra is our voice center. It is through our spoken word that we express ourselves to others. The healthfulness of this chakra is signified by how openly and honestly a person expresses himself or herself. A challenge to the throat chakra is for us to express ourselves in the most truthful manner. Speak your truth, lies will cause problems with this chakra. This behavior violates both our bodies and spirits. Repressing our selves instead of speaking up and communicating will manifest into throat imbalances such as strep throat, laryngitis, and speech impediments. We are powerful and can command what we need and affirm the positive, dispel the negative. We can be strong in our voice and confident.

Sixth Chakra: Ajna

Location: Brow

Color: Indigo

The third eye chakra is also called "brow chakra." The brow chakra that auric hues and other visual images are intuited clairvoyantly. Our mental calculations and thinking processes are functions of the third eye chakra. We are able to view life patterns and put them into perspective through the wisdom of the third chakra's actions. Our ability to separate reality from fantasy or delusion is connected to the healthfulness of this chakra. We can see the world and we can see the inner universe and see what is obscure to others.

Seventh Chakra: Sahasrara

Location: Top of Head

Color: White or Violet

The crown chakra allows inner communications with our spiritual nature to take place. The opening in the crown chakra serves as an entryway wherein the Universal Life Force can enter our bodies and be dispersed downward into the lower six chakras housed below it. This chakra when open represents spiritual awakening. The crown chakra could also be considered the bottomless well from which intuitive knowledge is drawn. We can receive energy from the universal and our communication is universal.

Tips, Techniques or Insights

It is essential to understand the chakras. There are more chakras such as the chakras in the palms sometimes called Buddha palms and the chakras on the bottom of the feet sometimes called the bubbling brook, but you can research them at a later date since there is a multitude of books and materials explaining them in detail. The chakras are vital to know because they do connect us to the Earths' energy, and to the universal energy, and it is equally valuable to know how they help with the energetic and healing systems between the individual and the universe. It is a good practice in the beginning to practice visualizing colors of chakras and or listening to music. Keep ourselves centered helps us to keep our chakras balanced. The importance of the chakras is vital to our health and wellbeing, and we should know the state of each in order to insure we are healthy. Our organs are affected by the health of our chakras since they receive vital energy via the Chakra system.

Chakra Colors

The Seven-Chakra System

Lesson Twenty-three:
Cultivating your Universe

Is there turmoil in your life, in your community, and in your country? Do you feel it? Have you watched the TV and seen war on TV? Have you been thinking about all the controversies, are you worried? Have you internalized some of the disorder and are there problems in your family that is creating more stress in your life such as bills and finances? This is happening at this time and it is requiring people to focus on being at peace and in harmony. Thinking of the higher qualities of life, we should focus on inner harmony and do not let outer turmoil destabilize our inner peace. Focus on the high ideals in life in order to keep from being impacted by the turmoil we witness outside in life and on TV.

Harmony

As we have discussed in many lessons, we discussed growing and healing not only ourselves but also others. We realize we are bigger than our own self and realize we are a link to the all, and the universal, so knowing this we can begin to realize that we can enter into harmony with our own inner self and then others. We share this planet with those close to us, and others throughout the universe.

The world and the stars and the planets appear to be in perfect harmony. Nature appears to be in harmony and when out of balance it corrects and comes back into equilibrium so that it will stay in harmony. We discussed the importance of balance within and without and knowing this we then learn how to stay in a state of harmony. It is essential to discern whether you are in harmony within and if not find out why you are not, and then correct yourself so that you are in accord on all levels. Harmony is most important within our own self through understanding that there is a harmony between heaven, man and the earth. This harmony is replicated within us as we integrate our inner self. As you sense or discern whether you are in harmony within also recognize if you are in harmony, in the universe. If not then perceive why not and correct that so you can enter into harmony with the universe. Recognize any discord and release from it. If it is not you release any discord coming from anywhere or anyone else. Affirm discord is not you, and remember the mind and heart should be in harmony.

Focus

As you move from the inner universe, then you can focus on the outer greater universe and receive all it is trying to provide for you. Remember you are more then just you as a part of this greater universe. Think carefully, what you are focusing on, is it the positive or the negative or things that do not matter. Am I focused on what's necessary to me so I can accomplish all I came here to do? Focus is crucial in terms of what comes first, second, third and etc. If healing you first is vital then focus on accomplishing that task. If helping others is your focus, then help others so you can accomplish that task. Also focus on being balanced, and centered all the time so that you are in harmony with the universe. Focus is how you accomplish goals. Lack of focus is how we do not achieve goals. We must always know where is our focus. Those who focus on peace do not create wars. Those who focus on wars do not create peace, they just more wars.

Peace

As you become calm and in harmony, you will feel a sense of inner peace. Outer peace is indispensable, but we never understand why there is not a lot of peace in the world because first within, their needs to be peace. As we grow we must learn to become peaceful within which is a feeling or sense of accomplishment. Understanding we are ok, all is well, and we can be happy within and not become discombobulated because the outer environment is not at ease, and dealing with some level of chaos and turmoil. We learn to understand the meaning, live and let live peaceably.

Inner peace is learning how to stay peaceful within no matter what's happening within the outer world at large. Some people think peace is given to you, but actually it is cultivated from knowing you are ok, all is well and in harmony. Do not let the outer world cause you to become in disharmony and un-centered. See that no matter what, you can be peaceful within and still deal with whatever is going on outside of us. We can learn how not to let negativity get inside to dishevel us. A happy home starts within a happy heart and stays with us when we are at peace. Peace is cultivated within and then permeates outward. War is the opposite of that. Inner peace is cultivated within you.

Tips, Techniques or Insights

Is everything in your life and the universe in harmony? Are you in harmony with your environment, if not why? Focus on what it would take to make your life in harmony. Are you focusing on harmony and inner peace or drama and dis-harmony? Contemplate on what's going on in your life. Envision what things you can implement to promote peace and harmony. Begin to let go of inharmonious thoughts. Let go of all discord. Focus on positive thinking and being around positive people and situations. Do things that promote peace and harmony in your life. Think about what makes you happy. Then if, you are not already doing these things begin to add and do things that make you happy, at ease and create harmony in your life. Remember when you are in harmony and at peace you are also in harmony with the universe. Strive for inner peace and inner harmony with the universal.

Lesson Twenty-four:
I have Learned My Lessons

If you pick the leaf of a tea plant and nurture the root you will continue to drink tea forever. If you pull the root or do not water the plant you will only have one cup of tea. You may learn to nurture your tea plants so you can grow and drink tea forever just as you must learn to nurture yourselves.

Experience

Are we learning? Yes, we are learning much is the key, but does it make us intelligent or wise? We learn many things from everywhere including what we see, hear and read. If I tell you the stove is hot, will you believe me, if you touch it will it convince you? Can you share that information with others? Will they understand you or believe you without touching the stove themselves? Some may believe you and others may have to touch the stove themselves to be convinced the stove is hot and not take your word on it. Do you really need to touch the stove is the question? The answer is both yes and no because some people learn by experiencing, and others learn by gaining insight or discernment and do not need to experience it to know what it is or not. By learning and experiencing things, you can use those experiences to teach and help others. Of course, the best we have learned, is "through our experiences" to know yourself first. In order to teach the student, you must first pass the course so what you learn is valuable for you and those you then turn to teach. So understanding that all we learn and experience gives us the opportunity to become wise. We can also learn to take wise advice.

Wisdom

There are accumulated experiences that help us to learn many lessons and help us to keep from repeating the same lesson over and over. There is wisdom of the ages that we gain and can access to help us with our lessons that we glean from all those around us such as ancestors, family and extended family and friends. This includes teachers and those we meet that impart wisdom to us when we need it. For spiritual people, we glean wisdom from our lessons and information we receive directly or indirectly, from the Divine and Spiritual Teachers who assist us in our spiritual growth. This is essential as our spiritual growth is teaching us many lessons and helping us to gain valuable insight and wisdom. Also doing our meditation helps us to gain valuable insight and inner wisdom and helps us gain wisdom from the universe. Wisdom comes from everywhere including nature and the universe. They are all our teachers, and as we grow inwardly as we learn how to gain and utilize the wisdom we glean from nature and the universe. Such things that are basic such as there is enough food to feed the world then why are people starving. Why would we pollute the air and water when it is vital to all life? As we understand these basic things we can understand there is no need for wars because wars do not create peace. Also, it is wise to be around positive, like-minded people. Trouble seeks its own reward, so we know we have to stay away from people who cause problems. You can grow in wisdom but learn nothing from a fool. A wise man can fish and an unwise man can only eat and saves nothing for a later date. Wisdom speaks fools do not listen. Being intelligent does not make you wise.

Tips, Techniques or Insights

So are you using what you have learned in your daily life? Is there something you are not doing that needs to be completed? Is anything repeating itself, continuing, that requires your attention? Meditate on what you are learning and seem not to be learning. Have you learned from your experiences and now use them to make the right decisions? Ask how are you using your wisdom to help you and help others? Ask yourself," am I making wise decisions", if so great if not begin to use your knowledge to make the right decisions. Meditate observe and listen to the universe to share its wisdom with you. Listen to your own innate wisdom. Seek out those who can help you such as an enlightened spiritual teacher.

Wisdom is given to us so that we can learn to make the right decisions after we have learned valuable lessons. If we have not learned our lessons well, had the wrong teachers, not used our wisdom wisely, and consistently make the wrong decisions then we have to learn more and realize that these experiences will continue to push us in the right direction until we learn to make the right decisions. Have no fear, begin to change and make the right decisions, seek the right teachers. We can start today. We want to become wise enough to help others to share in our knowledge and thereby helping them to make the right decisions. So you must always use your learnt knowledge wisely.

Lesson Twenty-five:
Universal Teachers

John was a multimillionaire and wanted to become a spiritual master and felt instead of researching, and learning from various Teachers he would just pay the highest level Spiritual Teacher he could find. He decided he to pay the Master Teacher 50 million dollars since he was exceedingly rich, and could afford to pay the Master to teach him all he needed to know to become a Spiritual Master. So John sought out the highest teacher in China, and after a brief search he was led to the highest Spiritual Teacher, on the highest Shan (mountain). So he ventured up to the top of the highest Shan, and when he got to the top of the mountain he went into the Temple, and asked to speak to the Highest Spiritual Teacher. The highest Teacher appeared and asked him how could he help him. John explained that he wanted to learn to become a spiritual master and would pay him $50 million dollars. The Teacher told him to keep his money, and he would teach him. The Teacher then told him to come back tomorrow to start learning at 6 am. John upon hearing this told the Teacher that he could not do it because he did not get up in the morning before 10 am. John returned home without learning anything. It is important to understand that when the student is ready the Teacher will appear. John thought he could buy the Master and really was not ready to be the student.

Angels

An Angel is defined as a supernatural being or spirit found in various religions and mythologies. They are often depicted as servants of God and celestial beings who act as intermediaries between heaven and Earth. In Zoroastrianism and Native American religions angels are depicted as a guiding influence or a guardian spirit. These spiritual beings or guardians are here to help us achieve and provide inspiration among other things to all whom they support. Angels represent qualities, virtues and powers of the Creator. Angels are pure energy and are here to represent higher consciousness that helps to transform people and the universe. Angels assist and help us to transfer our unconsciousness and consciousness to the highest level. If you want to know more do research and meditate about angels.

Guides

A guide is defined as a guru or spiritual person or spiritual guide that helps you to achieve a goal(s) or guides you on a path or helps you to accomplish tasks where it requires a guide or guru. There are many guides. Some of you are guides for your family. Most spiritual people have a spiritual guide(s) supporting them on their way, helping them to accomplish their goals and achieve success. Many guides help many spiritual people visibly and invisibly and are there whether you consciously realize it or not.

Teachers

Spiritual Teachers are defined as guides, gurus, advisors, and those who have the ability to teach you things or subjects that a person or student needs to learn. A teacher provides guidance for his or her students. There are many types of teachers. Some of you are teachers. Some of you are "in training" to become teachers and recognize your gift and opportunity to teach and help others. Teachers are available when you are ready and need them. Most high spiritual teachers have walked the path you are on, and have turned to help others by providing answers, wisdom, and inspiration to help all who come.

Spiritual Teachings

Spiritual teachings have been given to us to help us understand who we are, why we here, what we need to know and how to travel the path to spiritual enlightenment. There are numerous Spiritual Teachings that have been disseminated by living masters and spiritual teachers, and it is fortunate we can utilize them for vital spiritual resource information. Some of these are ancient such as Sutras, Vedas, Koran, and other numerous books. The ancient Sutras should be read and studied including other spiritual teachings, which can help you to advance on your spiritual path. There are too many Sutras to list, but you should research the Sutras and study them. Mahayana Sutras have been created in the Vedic, Buddhist, and Japanese philosophies and teachings to name a few. A synopsis of the Sutras can be read by obtaining a copy of the Mahayana Sutras, www.bookslic.net. This book covers 48 different sets of Sutras including such Sutras as the Golden Light Sutra, Diamond Sutra, the Heart Sutra, and the Lotus Sutra. There are many spiritual books and bibles (Psalms and Revelations for an example, Quran), some original, some have been rewritten to the point the original information is suspect but you should research spiritual teachings to learn what has been written to provide spiritual insight for us by Spiritual Masters.

Tips, Techniques or Insights

Many spiritual people have teachers, guides, angels that are assisting them and mankind to achieving their best including the healing and teaching of mankind. These spiritual beings are around us, and we can reach them in a variety of ways such as meditation, prayer, dreams, writing and etc.

To know who is around you, ask in you meditation or sit and ask, listen for the answer. Also consult spiritual advisors or guides or teachers around you. Know your angels, guides, and teachers', call to them in your meditation and they will respond if you are ready and are listening. There are other books and spiritual teachings written by Spiritual Teachers and Masters that will provide valuable insight and information. Be careful to make sure those who profess that they are spiritual teachers or advisors are only interested in assisting you and not trying to take advantage of you. When the student is ready the teacher will appear so respect the teacher!

Lesson Twenty-six:
Sharing and Serving the Universe

Jane was an extremely giving person who gave all she had to her family, friends and did all she could give year after year. She was immensely happy to give gifts to her extended family members and their children and to the neighborhood homeless people. Years later she wondered why she was alone, never married and she spent Christmas and New Years by herself. Her family invited her, but she did not want to be a burden. Her family asked her why she was that way and she said she loved giving but did not want to receive anything. When people offered her gifts, she refused to accept them telling everyone she did not need anything and only liked to give. She did this her whole life. Everyone called her benevolent. Now in her fifties she wondered why she met no one for a true loving relationship. Also, she noticed that even though she gave gifts she rarely got any (knowing she did not want any). One day she asked me what was wrong with her that it seemed she never received anything including a loving relationship. I explained to her that nothing was wrong except she could receive love if she would also be open to receiving. Not realizing this she had closed her heart to receiving, so when people tried to give her love, she refused to accept it. Giving is great, but you need to be open to receiving at the same time. She thought about it and realized that she did not mean to close her heart to receiving, she only wanted to give unconditionally without people thinking she was doing all she did for some reward. I told Jane that giving is great, and receiving is terrific also and that it would balance her and so she agreed, and within a year Jane met a charming guy and now she is in a good relationship.

Giving and Receiving

Giving and receiving are how we share the universe with others. We all want to receive whatever we need and expect this and more. We expect to receive what we need but also want what we see. This is considered getting what we want whether or not it is needed. Some call it part of our ability to acquire and some have acquired much while some people have acquired very little. We expect to receive the basic needs that all humans require such as food, shelter and clothing. Once the basic needs are fulfilled then we expect to receive other intrinsic needs such as love, and other spiritual needs. This is what makes us grow and prosper on many different levels. This is expected even though some receive a lot; some unfortunately, receive very little. After we receive all we need and require some people also give and share what they have received with others not so fortunate. This helps those deprived and/or underserved by society for various reasons. This giving is effortless to the expansive and many who have received so much, so they give back to those in need. Giving can be as easy as sharing information, food, shelter, insight, wisdom, money and love. Yes, those who give and receive also share their love in relationships.

Love also comes within selfless love or compassion, which is giving without expecting anything in return. Giving expecting something in return is just trading it is not compassion. Giving selflessly is how compassionate people share things physical and intrinsic in order to help others, and provide service to all mankind.

Selfless Service

Part and parcel of giving and receiving is all part of living in this universe, but we must also understand that it is also encompassed within compassionate hearts that create a compassionate universe, and a part of that is providing selfless service. Light-workers, healers and many spiritual people provide essential services that go beyond their own individual needs, to help others including underserved populations and sometimes this is a part of their fulfillment to share whatever they have small or large with others. Selfless service is essential, and many can help by doing their small or a substantial part. Helping one person is helping a generation so do not think "my small contribution is too little", as it all counts. So if, you are called to provide service give selflessly and know that you are a universal service worker, and whatever you do is worth it. Money is not the only answer. Showing love is priceless to those deprived of basic caring and nurturing, so "do your part whatever that part may be".

Tips, Techniques or Insights

Giving is an art, but receiving Is also an art, and this is where sometimes the in-balance can happen by those who receive and give and not at the same time. Then there are those who give all the time but do not allow themselves to receive at the same time. Then there are those who receive all the time but think it is all for them only, and no need to share. Of course, there are those who want it all and to receive it all and more which contributes to greed and they will not share. Then there are those who give it all and end up with nothing because they have never received or are around only takers. Whatever the situation it is ideal to give and receive so that we can be balanced and know we all can share this universe together.

If you are serving mankind keep up the good work. There is a multitude of ways to serve mankind such as healers, guides, advisors, teachers, light workers, and etc. if you want to serve mankind then start and know that you are doing the right thing because we all can serve in some way. If you do not know how and what to do seek an advisor, meditate to see what is the best way for you to contribute. We all have something to share. We can also give selflessly by sharing compassion to others who need it.

Sahararar Crown Chakra Seventh Chakra

The opening in the crown chakra serves as an entryway wherein
the Universal Life Force can enter our bodies and be dispersed
downward into the lower six chakras housed below it

Lesson Twenty-seven:
Nirvana

Once a man wanted to reach the highest level of Enlightenment, and he heard that there are Gurus' who have reached this level and could help him to realize that state called Nirvana. So he thought, "I will just go to India and find the highest Guru and tell him to Enlighten me". So he flew to India and traveled around looking for the highest Guru. He asked several people who was the highest Guru and where did he live. Finally, they told him the highest Guru lived on top of a mountain. So he began to trek up to the top of the mountain, and when he got to the top he saw a temple and banged on the door. He hollered "for the Guru" to open the door. The door suddenly opened, and the Highest Guru looked at him and asked him "why have you come". The young man explained that he had come so he could be Enlightened. The man asked the Guru to enlighten him. The Guru slapped his face and then said, "Ok, now go back home". Motto is, it requires more than just a request, and you have to achieve it. The path is within you along with the mountain to climb.

Enlightenment

Enlightenment is defined as a final, blessed state free from ignorance, desire and suffering. It is a state of awakened consciousness that some call Nirvana. It is the path of those who are walking the path of Light and are serious about obtaining this level and ready to do what it requires.

Nirvana is defined as freedom from the endless cycle of personal reincarnations, with their consequent suffering, as a result of the extinction of personal passion, hatred, and delusion: attained by the Arhat as his goal but postponed by the Bodhisattva. It is also considered being a place or state whereby one is characterized by freedom from or oblivion to pain, worry, and the external world. These definitions are based on a known awareness and esoteric knowledge of what a spiritual person has attained as they reach a pinnacle in the walk of their spiritual path. To understand the meaning of enlightenment, you have to live it, experience it, achieve it then you know it, and have reached a pinnacle of your spiritual growth. Nirvana is a term for reaching perfect enlightenment that many spiritual people strive towards and many Buddha's reach. You can read about many Masters who have achieved this level and they can explain to you what they achieved, but it is better understood after you have reached this stage of development on your own. This can be obtained in this lifetime if you are genuine and do what it takes to achieve this goal.

Tips, Techniques or Insights

How to reach this goal is the question. First you need to ask if you can achieve this goal and if you are ready to do what it takes. Second you need to begin to sit and meditate on what is required. Consult the Higher Source. Thirdly you will need to listen and find a competent Enlightened Teacher. Fourth, this book begins to help you to see beyond the physical, the mental to focus your attention toward the inner universe and the higher universe. As you contemplate the universe, you will see the path before you and know how to move toward that quest and how to arrive there. If you seek, and ask questions and are open to receive you will know the answer. Also, the Mahayana Sutras such as the Lotus Sutra discuss Nirvana and how to attain perfect spiritual enlightenment so study them.

Addendum Contemplate this:

IS ALL OK WITH YOUR WORLD, YOUR UNIVERSE

Is all ok with the world?

Is all ok with your world? If yes then you have no argument, no gripe, nothing to cry about, unless you are inclined to make up stuff in your own bag with drama.

Are you desperately seeking something you can touch, can see, feel or are you seeking the mysterious, the invisible the unknown. Does the dream keep you up at night or are you awake, and sleepwalking when you should be asleep? These are only questions of the dilemma we sometimes find ourselves enveloped and that occupy our minds whether we are awake or sleep. Maybe, all of this is just a challenge or an opportunity for us, to learn by making us become or appear to be desperate for whatever we think or feel we need or appears to be missing in our life

Causation Versus Symptom.

The cause is greater than the symptom, but most of the time, we tend to treat only the symptom until it gets out of control or it appears to us that it cannot be fixed. What we continue not to realize is the symptom is sounding an alarm that there is something we need to pay attention. It gets louder, so we need to listen and correct the problem or challenge no matter what it is. In order to do this, we must go beyond the symptom, and find the source in order to cure the problem or challenge and prove we have learned the lesson.

The question is, without looking, how can we see the forest from the trees.

We need to look, listen, seek the right advice, at the right time, and not try to hide, hoping it will go away. There is a solution for everything if we dare or care to seek out the answer. As a Healer, we must seek out answers that appear not to be there but are hidden just below the surface of our consciousness, waiting there, similar to how we wait for the knock on the door from an expected friend. The healer does not have the luxury only to treat the cut on the hand or the bruise on the leg or the pain in the gut, but the Healer is required to go where no one else will go and find the cause so that the proper advice, the proper prescription, the appropriate solution will correct the problem. The Healer seeks to heal the challenge, in order to seize the opportunity for his or her client and take advantage to change the course of the person's life helping them to grow and learn at the same time.

The Opportunity.

This is the opportunity to be healed, but for the Healer the healing has already happened because there is no dis-ease, no sickness but only a challenge, an opportunity for higher knowledge that will help the student to complete their lessons. So learning is continuous, and we learn many lessons during our lifetime.

I work with those who have chosen a path of helping others, but first must help their self. I help those who need to realize their goals of higher learning or growth with skills and gifts that have been bestowed upon them by a Higher Source. These gifts or skills are given to help them to grow and learn, and one day be ready and able to teach others or inspire others to do the same.

How do we help others?

The best way is first to listen because there is always a higher source, higher ideal, higher voice operating if we just listen. There are those who have come to help those who need to hear, want to hear, care to listen and help themselves as well as others. For some, there is a Voice, that Higher Source calling to them to heal and be well. If you cannot hear or see or feel then, you must seek out those who listen, who see, who feel who are here to help you through those times that appear to be desperate. Where the wall appears to be larger than the house, where the problem is bigger than the rock so that you can receive their guidance, healing, and learning so you can do and know this is true.

Is it worth your time and effort? Yes,

Growth, learning is worth every effort especially in an experiential world that we make as our home. There is light at the end of the tunnel if you will use your vision. If you cannot then it is time to seek out those that have the vision and the Light and can see beyond the problems to where a state of bliss exists for you and everyone else. It is possible to learn, to grow and be well. I train and teach healers, light workers, coaches, guides and those who seek higher guidance, higher vision, higher hearing than the noise next door or in the street, cars screeching on their way to where they need to go. I work with those whom only desperation is the call to higher learning, to a higher journey who need to clear away the clouds of misunderstanding and confusion to see their clear path out of the wilderness into the Light.

Who is here to help you?

I am here to help you so that you will be ok, help others to be ok, and then the world will be ok with you and visa versa. We cannot leave you behind, but you must seek to question, ask to know, try to find out, ask the right person and by all means have faith and trust that you will get the right answers. Also getting the correct information, the proper guidance that will heal you, help you, guide you, teach you in order for you then to turn, and share your wisdom and advice so others also may heal perfectly! Many are now being called to wake up and know whom you are and learn about you and what you need to know. At the Spiritual Life Source Center, we will help you to be all you can be that is best! We help you local or long distance. I can be reached at the Spiritual Life Source Center.

Index

In "The Song of Life" we begin to awaken a sense of the universal, the healing within you to let you know you are not done if you haven't explored the universal and seen yourself, and as a part of the universe. Yes you can heal you but stopping there you are not all done. I want to heal the universe and we are a part of the universe and we want the universe healed for all of us who realize we all are a part, realizing the Sun shines on us to awaken us to the light.

The Song of Life provides tips and insights to assist you to gain valuable knowledge, techniques and assistance to spur you on to greater understanding of you and your universe. The Song of Life begins to awaken a sense of the universal, the healing within you to let you know you are not done if you haven't explored the universal and seen yourself as a part of the universe delve within.

The Author and the Teacher

The author George Samuels is an enlightened realized Spiritual Master, Guide, Teacher, Healer, Spiritual Coach and Poet living in the San Diego area and is here to teach and help heal those who seek answers and to learn in order to help others. Master George has been providing

Light, spiritual wisdom, healing, coaching and spiritual guidance for thousands of people throughout the USA and other countries for more than 30 years. He is continues and is currently helping and healing all who contact him and are seeking Light on the Path. George has written several books of poetry such as "Audacity of Poetry", "Healing in a Word", "With Poetry in Mind", "This is Our Word" and "There is Only Music Brother", "Doors to Ancient poetical Echoes" and "Lovers Should never Quarrel". His websites are www.spirituallifesource.com *and* www.gsamuelsbooksandart.com